STEPHENS COLLEGE
COLUMBIA, MO.

DISCA

D1624583

THE FATHER OF LITTLE WOMEN

STEPHENS COLLEGE
LIBRARY

A. BRONSON ALCOTT

STEPHENS COLLEGE
LIBRARY

THE FATHER
OF LITTLE WOMEN

BY

HONORÉ WILLSIE MORROW

WITH ILLUSTRATIONS

BOSTON
LITTLE, BROWN, AND COMPANY
1927

7 999

Copyright, 1925, 1926, 1927,
By Wolsey Pratt

———

All rights reserved

Published September, 1927
Reprinted November, 1927

Printed in the United States of America

PS
1014
.M6

Contents

v

CONTENTS

Illustrations

STEPHENS COLLEGE
LIBRARY

THE FATHER OF LITTLE WOMEN

CHAPTER I

Explanatory and Personal

THIS is in no sense a biography. It is merely an attempt to retrieve something infinitely precious that has long been mislaid in America: namely Bronson Alcott's theory of the best method to educate young children.

I will admit at the start that intellectually I do not flatter myself that I'm peculiarly fit for the task of paraphrasing Mr. Alcott's theories. On the other hand, I seem to be the only one interested in them up to the present, and moreover, I inherited that interest. My mother was a New Englander who spent her married life in the Middle West and who was always homesick for the land that had bred her. One of her solaces was to talk to us about the men and women she had known in her girlhood.

One of my dearest memories of her is of the winter twilights when, rocking my little sister in her arms before the old "base burner" she talked to us about the picture that hung beside the engraving of Daniel Webster. It was a tiny water color of a moss rosebud in a narrow blue frame. There was a series of stories connected with that picture, for which we children asked again and again : for it was the work of Abba May Alcott, the Amy of "Little Women." My mother had taken painting lessons from Miss Alcott, when she was a little girl. She had many a tale to tell, of the gayety and charm of May and of her really fine talent, "which," Mother always added firmly, "she inherited from her father and not from her mother. Mrs. Alcott was always given the credit for what Louisa and the others amounted to. But my father always said that Bronson Alcott, their father, was a very great genius, born a hundred years before his time. And I believe that both Louisa and Abba May got their great talents from their father."

In the telling of what we called her Amy stories, Mother repeated this statement many times, and at last I grew up sufficiently to ask her why she always stressed it so. "Because," she said, "I believe that Harriet Martineau, when she ridiculed Mr. Alcott's King's Chapel School in Boston out of existence, set back the clock for education not only in this country but in the world, a hundred years.

4

I remember Bronson Alcott vividly. When I was a girl and he came to Exeter to lecture, he used to stop at our house. I can remember that I thought him the most beautiful man to look at and the most fascinating talker that I had known or ever would know. And I still think so. And I'd like to see justice done him."

"Yes, and what of that?" I asked with the nonchalance of youth and ignorance.

"What of that?" flared Mother. "What of anything that impedes the nation's growth? Bronson Alcott would have been one of the greatest glories of New England and they would n't have it. They crucified him. They laughed at him as an impractical visionary, a man who allowed his family to go hungry while he dreamed dreams. Every one but Emerson. Emerson understood him and was not above drawing on him for philosophical sustenance. Never forget that."

And you observe by this that I have not! But many, many years of living and loss, and mental and physical travail were to go by before Mother's words were to come back to me with their full significance.

As I grow older, nothing astonishes me so much as the inexplicable continuity of apparently irrelevant events in one's life. There is my dear Mother in the Middle West with her unquenchable enthusiasm for the older giants of New England, and her unceasing partisanship of Bronson Alcott, and there is, many, many years later, an editor who asks me to write an account of Bronson Alcott as the father of the author of what is still the most popular book for young people ever written, "Little Women." This editor had heard that Bronson Alcott had left behind him an unpublished diary. Perhaps this diary might contain some interesting references to Louisa May Alcott.

As the editor spoke of this, the clock of memory struck! I was sitting at my Mother's knee, looking at a moss rosebud in a blue frame "Perhaps," I ventured, "Bronson Alcott might be interesting for himself, because of his theories of education."

The editor was a little doubtful, as I was. But his suggestion interested me and after learning that the diary was supposed to be still in the Alcott home in Concord, Massachusetts, I started on what proved to be the most charming literary adventure of my life.

I found the diary. It consists of some fifty volumes of exquisite handwriting on yellowed paper. Each volume contains three hundred odd pages. The books are handsomely bound. Louisa had this done for her father when her earnings from "Little Women" and the other immortal juveniles made it possible. Bronson began to keep his diary, or journal as he calls it, when he was in his early twenties. He was born in 1799 and died in 1888, and kept up his journals to the end.

Here, then, to my hand, was the record of almost fifty years of a scholarly man's life; fifty years of the most critical period of America's life. Why had it gone unpublished all these years? Again my memory spoke. Mother had said that he was hooted down as an impractical visionary. Inquiry proved her statement still true. The mention of Bronson Alcott's name to any one to whom the name means anything, brings a smile of derision, to-day — a philosophical fool — a lazy dreamer; it was his wife who made Louisa what she was. The diaries? Yes, but they are like the man, impossible. He never wrote of outward happenings. He was interested only in the growth of his own philosophy.

Certainly the reports and comments were not enticing. Nevertheless, those tall, brown books drew me. Perhaps the atmosphere of Bronson

Alcott's library in which they repose, drew me too. It is such a room as time and New England alone can produce. In all the far West, in all the Middle West or South, there could be no such room because the culture there lacks the material austerity and the mental richness that created Bronson Alcott's library. A square room with windows on opposite sides, and a small marble-faced fireplace, inconspicuous in design. Worn old chairs and reading lamps, and round the walls bookshelves, crowded with books. Books overflowing the cases to tables. The bust of Socrates, of Bronson Alcott and of Louisa. Tiny choice portraits of the Alcotts, a program for a child's day of work and play in faded ink, and on my first day there the snow slashing against the windows, the glow of firelight on the rich bindings of old books. This had been Thoreau's home and then Bronson Alcott's. Louisa had bought it for her father and mother after her success had become assured.

In this room, it seemed a natural thing to open and read the Journals. Difficult reading, indeed. The beauty of the writing was all in appearance. It was hard to decipher. Moreover, it dealt, as I had been warned, only casually with outward events with which I could be to some degree famil-

8

STEPHENS COLLEGE
LIBRARY

Order of In-door Duties

for Children.

Sept 1846

Morning	Forenoon	Noon	Afternoon	Evening
5. Rise, Bathe, Dress.	9. Studies with Mr Lane.	12. Dinner	1. Rest.	6. Supper. Recreation. Conversation. Music.
6. Breakfast Housewifery Recreations (Chores) in care of Miss Ford	10½. Recreations. 11. Studies with Father		2. Sewing Conversation and Reading with Mother and Miss Ford. 4. Errands and (Chores) Recreations.	8. 8½. Bed.

Vigilance, Punctuality, Perseverance.

Prompt, Cheerful, Unquestioning, Obedience.

Government of Temper, Hands, and Tongue.

Gentle Manners, Motions, and Words.

Work, Studies, and Play distinct.

No interchange of Labors.

Bathing Hours 5. - 10½ - 5.

Study Hours 9. 10½. 11 to 12.

Observe Silence and Stillness.

Labor Hours	6½ to 8.	2 to 4.
Play Hours	8 to 9. 10 to 10½. 4 to 6	
Eating Hours	6. 6½. 12. 12½. 6. 6½.	
Sleeping Hours	8 to 5. 8½ to 5.	

MR. ALCOTT'S CHART OF THE CHILDREN'S
INDOOR DUTIES

iar. For a time, I skipped from book to book, seeking for some known landmark by which to orient myself. Perhaps the man had nothing human to offer, after all. Suddenly, I paused. On a page was the delicate outline of a child's hand and a label. "Louisa's hand. Aged two years." That little hand led me as surely as a signpost to the adjacent page, and I discovered that I was reading a masterly psychological study of the baby mind of Louisa May Alcott. A study so modern that it might have been written yesterday. And with this discovery, my vacillating ceased. The diaries became living entities to me and out of them grew before my fascinated vision a giant who had been lost, a star that no telescope had been strong enough to bring into our ken.

Bronson Alcott was and is the greatest of all America's schoolmasters. It is as a schoolmaster, as a genius who attempted to remake America's ideas of the functions of education, that I have dealt with him in the pages that follow. We have immediate and enormous need of such a genius to-day. Until we recognize him, if he exists, any teacher, any parent cannot afford to miss an understanding of what Bronson Alcott tried to do.

I am taking it for granted that you who read these pages are, as I am, a product of the American Public School System. So that when I cite my own spiritual starvation in school, you, I believe, are going to understand and feel as I do.

Looking back over my years from the primary grade to the last year in the high school, I cannot recall a single effort on the part of my teachers to develop the spiritual part of my mind. Our schools were regarded jealously by the different religious denominations of the State. Methodists, Catholics, Baptists, Unitarians, Lutherans, Presbyterians and Jews — all the sects and creeds representing men's varying minds saw to it that there was absolute religious freedom in the public schools. As a consequence we had no religion at all.

My teachers were of all denominations. The two that affected me most profoundly, intellectually, were, one, a Catholic, the other, a Presbyterian. I cannot recall either of them even mentioning spiritual matters to me. They dared not. Had they done so, some one would have raised the howl: "The Catholics or the Presbyterians are getting a foothold in the schools!" and dire political consequences would have resulted. Except in some casual literary or historical reference, the Bible never was mentioned. I do not recall ever having heard a prayer in school.

In other words, the American public school makes a complete cleavage between the growth and the training of the soul and the growth and training of the brain. Whatever I got of spiritual development during the plastic and most important years of my life, I had to gather as a by-product for myself from my school studies. There was Sunday school for an hour, once a week! If your Sunday school did for you what it did for me, its influence on your life is negligible!

The real problem of America's education to-day is not what intellectual food we shall give our children. The real problem is where shall we find spiritual food for them. The future of America rests on the answer we find to this query. Until I studied the ideas and ideals of Bronson Alcott, I had no hope of coming upon a practical solution to the problem. Myself — I have no equipment for handling the menacing perplexities of behavior.

Nothing in all my years at school had to do with things of the spirit — with matters of the soul's ideals related to the conduct of the mind and body. Years and years of my school life on the multiplication table, on parsing Gray's "Elegy in a Country Churchyard", on translating *Arma virumque cano* — not fifteen minutes on Who is God and How Responsible am I to Him?

I repeat, we have need of a genius to remake our ideas of the function of education. Over a hundred years ago such a genius stood before his uncle in Cheshire, a pink-cheeked, troubled boy of thirteen, and begged for the chance to develop his soul along with his mind and the uncle could understand no better then than we could to-day. He was starving, that youngster, just as we were starved as children, and just as we are starving our children now. The difference is that he was an intellectual giant and knew he was being starved and we never dreamed of such a thing.

In presenting Alcott's ideas and ideals, I have as much as possible allowed him to speak for himself. I have made no attempt to account for him. All the psychoanalysis known to our finest specialists never yet has accounted for genius. What Emerson said of Bronson is as nearly adequate a statement of the man's powers as we can hope to find. Why the powers, only that Universal Spirit which Bronson understood better than the rest of us, could say:

Last night in the conversation, Alcott appeared to great advantage and I saw again as often before, his singular superiority. As pure intellect, I never have seen his equal. The people interrupt him with "Do you know, Mr. Alcott, I think thus and so," and do not know that they have interrupted his large and progressive statement; do not know that all they have in their baby brains is incoherent and spotty; that all he sees and says is like astronomy, lying there real and vast, and every part in eternal connection with the whole, and that they ought to sit in silent gratitude, eager only to hear more. The moral benefit of such a mind cannot be told. The world fades; men, reputations, politics shrivel. The interests, power, future of the soul beam a new day — Spring! Faith becomes sight — He is the most extraordinary man and the highest genius of the time. He is a man. He is erect. He sees, let whoever be overthrown or parasitic or blind.

CHAPTER II

The Beginning of Bronson Alcott

NOTHING is so tragic about the disappearance of the New England leaven from American life as the fact that New England itself destroyed so much of that leaven. And the story of Bronson Alcott tells, as nothing else can tell, how New England killed the things it loved.

Although Bronson's father and mother were hard-working farmer folk, they came of distinguished stock, Anglo-Saxon on both sides. One of the earlier Alcotts was Lord Chancellor of England. His descendant, John Alcott, was graduated from Harvard College in 1646 and was first a schoolmaster and afterward a physician. He was granted a farm of a thousand acres near Boston by the Honorable General Court of Massachusetts "in consideration of many long services discharged for his country as also of other services." Sons and daughters of this John married governors and diplomats and men and women distinguished for their love of letters. One of these sons was Bron-

son's great-grandfather, a Yale graduate, who
hewed out of the Connecticut wilderness, twenty-
five miles north of New Haven, a farm of a thousand acres. His grandson, Joseph, married Anna
Bronson, the daughter of a well-known and stanch
Episcopalian, Amos Bronson, and so the little
boy who was to become the "Father March" of
"Little Women" was named Amos Bronson Alcott.
He was born on his father's farm on Spindle
Hill, near Wolcott, Connecticut, November 29,
1799.

He was a very beautiful little boy with blue eyes
and yellow hair, a slender, serious face and lips
that had humorous corners. It was a good-look-
ing family though, and it was probably not his
beauty that made him rather the favorite of her
nine children with his mother. To these other
children, husky, hard-working, hard-playing, inde-
pendent farm children, she gave, of course, all a
mother's devotion, but little Bronson, from babyhood, was different : a quiet child with a quiet
passion for beauty and for matters of the mind
that his brothers and sisters did not show. And
because she herself yearned for books and beauty,
Bronson's mother was delighted that one of her
children shared her feeling and she did all that she

could to help the boy to scholarly attainments. But this, in the Spindle Hill of those days, was all but prohibitively difficult.

The Alcott farm, beautiful though it was on its hill top, required all the labor of all the family to wrest from it even the simple living of those primitive days: plowing, reaping, threshing, spinning, weaving, wood-cutting, preparing during all the warm months for the heavy siege of winter, preparing during the winter the clothing and the farm implements that would be needed during the warm weather. Life was a continual round of heavy manual labor, and except for church on Sundays and the husking bees and quilting parties, there was little leisure for social intercourse and almost none for intellectual. The Alcotts were not more hard-working than their neighbors. It was a pioneer period wherein things of the mind had to lie dormant.

But even as a very little fellow, Bronson could not be content with his small chores and crude games. One winter's day, his mother kept him long beside her, handing the warping threads for the reed as she wove the web in her loom. He was a patient little chap but as the shadows grew heavy in the great raftered kitchen, he protested.

"I don't like this, Mother. I'd rather have you tell me stories."

"I've told you all my stories, little son," replied his mother.

"I wish they were all written down and that I could read them for myself," sighed the small Bronson.

"A sensible wish for you that can neither read nor write, and are too little to go to the school-house!" smiled his mother.

"But if I had paper and a pen I could try. I could make marks, I could!" Bronson forgot his task and stared up into his mother's face, eyes blazing with ambition.

His mother shook her head. "The pen I could give you, but the paper, no." Then as if she could not bear the look of disappointment in the blue eyes, she suggested, "Why not a nicely sharpened piece of charcoal and the clean floor here beside the loom?"

The child dashed to the fireplace and returned with a bit of charcoal. His mother descended from the loom and the two knelt on the floor. "A a, B b, C c."

The weaving was forgotten. The fire burned low. The westering light in the kitchen window changed from crimson to pink. Soon the men of the household would come in from their chores, starving for supper, and supper would be late. But that did not matter. The child who was to grow into the greatest teacher in America was receiving his first lesson in his A B C's.

From that day on for weeks, the hours at weaving and spinning, hitherto such dragging chores, became the great hours of the day for mother and son, now teacher and pupil. The child galloped through the New England primer. "In Adam's Fall, We Sinned All." "The Eagle's Flight is Out of Sight." Then he clamored for more. There was the Bible, the Almanac; little else. His mother talked the matter over with his father. Little as he was, she felt Bronson must go to school. It would be as wicked a thing, she said, to starve that hungry mind as it would be to deprive him of food. And so the child, small as he was to attempt school in the midst of a Connecticut winter, was allowed to fight his way through the two miles of drifts to the crossroads schoolhouse.

Because he was one day to show Connecticut a revolutionized type of schoolroom, and because this schoolhouse was typical of Connecticut and all the rest of New England at that time, Bronson's description of it has peculiar interest. The little building, he says, was about twenty feet square, with a huge fireplace and tiny entry at one end. Crude desks and benches comprised the furniture. In severe weather about a cord of wood a week was burned in the fireplace, but the wood was always left in the road and buried in snow and burned both wet and green, so that in cold weather the air was almost unendurable. Men teachers, at a salary of seven to eleven dollars a month, were employed in winter; women at from two and a half to four dollars a month in summer. Writing and spelling were leading studies every day, and on Saturday, the old Assembly Catechism in the Congregational and in the Episcopal order were repeated regularly. Webster's Spelling Book, the American Preceptor and the New Testament were the principal books used. Arithmetic was taught one or two evenings a week.

So picture to yourself little Bronson, at five, panting down the long hill from the farm to the schoolhouse and standing abashed just within the door as school was called, too frightened to take off cap or mittens or his father's huge knit scarf in which his mother has swaddled him; too frightened to tell the teacher his name, or to wipe his little red nose or to heed the children tittering at him; but not so frightened that his small heart did not thrill when he saw the half dozen books on the teacher's desk. Books!

Amos Bronson Alcott, aged 5. He was seated on the front bench beneath the teacher's eye with the half dozen other wriggling young sculpins of the first class, not a pocket handkerchief among the crew. And after the teacher had prepared many pens for many children with chilblained fingers, after a dozen bottles of homemade ink had been thawed out at the blazing fire, after the teacher had set innumerable copies on papers and slates, after the second class had read stumblingly from the Gospel of St. Luke, and the third and fourth classes had spelled by heart the long columns of astounding and unheard-of words, the master called the little first class before his desk. They came with their primers and slates. Bronson, the tiniest and the newcomer, at the foot of the class.

The five before Bronson spelled laboriously through a sentence each. It was Bronson's turn. Blushing, in a tiny treble voice, he read his sentence without hesitation. The schoolmaster turned a rapid page or two and pointed to a little fable.

Bronson read it without an error, face crimson, blue eyes filled with tears of embarrassment. The master, a staid young man preparing for the ministry, looked at the small boy with a brightening eye.

"How far have you gone in the primer, Bronson ?"

"Through it, please, sir!" guiltily, from the child.

"Have you read anything else ?" The school was all attention, even the loutish chaps of fifteen listening.

"The 1804 Almanac and some of the Gospels," whispered Bronson.

The master opened his Bible to the lesson over which the second class had been stumbling and pointed with his quill pen. "Read this if you can, Bronson."

And the child read clearly, without hesitation. "There was in the days of Herod, the king of Judea, a certain priest named Zacharias, of the course of Abia. . . ." And on and on, through whatever passages the master showed him. Finally the master took the book from him and said, "You will read with the top class. Can you spell ?"

"Only through the primer," replied Bronson.

"You will spell with the second class. Can you write?"

"Yes, sir. Mother taught me on the floor." He stood at the master's desk, pink tongue caught in the corner of his mouth and with his little chapped fist clasping the slate pencil wrote without copy, "GOD is Love."

The master stared at the huge, graceful letters and sighed from sheer pleasure. "You will write with the top class."

And so the small Bronson launched his school career. One must pick the story of this with great patience from his later diaries, from his letters to his daughters, to his mother, from notes on his later writings. Mostly it is a story of hardship and of unbelievable yearning and striving for the finer things of life. It may be guessed that in a few terms of the district school he practically had exhausted its resources, and he began to look about him for other intellectual worlds to conquer. There were a few books in the neighborhood and Bronson borrowed them one after another. He read them winter evenings before the fire, while his mother knitted and his father worked out hickory ax helves. He read them in the spring when, set to weed the garden, he conscientiously did his stint, but at the rest periods he allowed himself, at the end of the rows, he buried himself in some treasury of words. Thus before he was twelve he had read through this small but astounding list: Young's "Night Thoughts", Milton's "Paradise Lost", "Robinson Crusoe", Burgh's "Dignity of Human Nature", Herney's "Meditations", Thompson's "Seasons." Then on a certain unforgettable day he borrowed a copy of Bunyan's "Pilgrim's Progress."

O charming story! he records. My haunts by meadow, rock and brook were made by it enchanted ground. It would be disloyal to myself and the author did I not record my early interest in this delightful allegory, the charm it had for me when a boy, the ideal of life which its perusal awoke and fostered in me, afar from books and the haunts of cultivated people. More than any work of genius, more than all other books, the Dreamer's Dream brought me into a living acquaintance with myself, my duties; and if the value of work is to be determined by its power to interest and to educate its readers, then I must acknowledge my debt to be the greatest to the author of Pilgrim's Progress.

He borrowed it again and yet again, copied whole chapters to keep with him when he could not have the book and often, he says, left the oxen and the plow standing in the furrow while, sitting on the wall beside the field, he enacted the drama of that most dramatic book, himself taking the part of Christian.

You will recall that the Little Women loved nothing better than to impersonate the trials of the unforgettable Christian. Whoever loaned the book first to Bronson dropped a pebble into deep waters, the concentric rings of which were not to cease rippling for a hundred years.

Bunyan gave a focus to the profoundly spiritual trend of the boy's mind. His mother's brother was the rector of St. John's, a tiny Episcopal church at Waterbury, and Mrs. Alcott hoped that Bronson would follow in his uncle's footsteps. The little boy used to ride with his mother on horseback the four miles to St. John's, and he records with what excitement he first saw a church with a steeple and how deeply he was impressed by the beauty of the service. Yet much as she desired that he enter the ministry, his mother did not try to force the boy's decision. His diary records :

I have reason to be grateful to my parents for leaving me free to choose and fashion a religious faith in accordance with my native temperament and gifts. I was taught to reverence and speak the truth and practice personal purity. I was taught at school to recite the Westminster and Episcopal Catechisms. In the formation of my religious views I am not aware of being permanently influenced by any of my contemporaries. There is a spiritual as there is a human heredity, a family creed and likeness.

Though he dreamed of being a clergyman, in a general way, Bronson's thoughts from the time he was eleven or twelve and had exhausted the mental stores of the district school, were on how and where he was to get an education. There was no money to send him anywhere. He had read and reread all the books in the neighborhood. He worked very hard at the heavy routine of farm chores, worked uncomplainingly as his conscientious nature dictated, but was all the time afflicted by a restlessness and a yearning for a gentler life that was far too precocious for a boy of twelve. Only his mother understood and sympathized, for bound like a galley slave to the heavy, ceaseless labors of the farm wife, she too longed silently for the things that belonged to the brain and not to the body.

25

When he was thirteen, his uncle, then living in Cheshire, Connecticut, invited Bronson to spend the winter with him acting as errand boy and helper while he attended the district school. It seemed like an overwhelmingly fine opportunity, and great were the preparations made by Mrs. Alcott to send the boy away well provided with clothes. He made the twelve-mile trip, thrilled by the wonder of his going and feeling that the career of scholar was now assured to him. But at Cheshire a curiously significant situation developed.

The boys and girls of Cheshire made fun of the quiet country boy. Even his beauty became the butt of their imbecilic wit. Bronson was homesick, but more than that, he was deeply disappointed in the school itself. He tried to explain this to his uncle.

"It's all show, sir. They learn everything by rote just as we did at Spindle Hill."

"But how else would they learn?" demanded his astounded uncle, gazing at his godson with a little resentment.

Bronson, tall for his thirteen years, his cheeks pink and his fine blue eyes still with the sweetness and innocence of childhood in their depths, struggled with an idea only half formed and much too big for his years.

"What's the use, Uncle, of learning by rote when you don't understand it? I can learn words by myself. What I want the teacher to show me is how to understand things!"

"But the teacher will explain anything you ask about," declared his uncle.

Bronson shook his blond head, made several attempts and finally said in his halting, gentle way, "What I want the teacher to do is to train the thing that I understand with, so he won't have to explain what's in the lesson books."

"You'd better get in the wood for the evening and not criticize your betters," said Bronson's uncle.

"I've done my chores," replied the boy. "What I want to ask you, sir, is your permission to stop going to school and spend my time reading here in your library."

Uncle Tillotson's good ministerial jaw almost clanked against his white frilled shirt front. "Why, you ungrateful young fool! Most certainly not! What childish evasion is this? Are you not the boy who is supposed to be eager for an education? Let's hear no more of this nonsense, Bronson."

27

Bronson's lips quivered and he made a move that was to be characteristic of all the rest of his beautiful, thwarted life.

"But, Uncle, I can educate myself, if you will give me leave to read all your books. And — and — if you don't give me leave, I — I shall go back home. For I don't want to be away from — from mother and deprive father of my help on the farm just to have my memory trained."

His uncle's voice was stern. It was a day when children were not allowed to express their preference.

"You will return home then, to-morrow. When you are ready to take the discipline to which other children submit themselves you may return."

But Bronson did not wait until morning. He fled to his cold little attic room, tied up his possessions in a gray shawl which he slung from his shoulder, and fled out into the afterglow, over the drifted roads toward home. It was bitter cold, the roads were poor at best, and now waist-deep in spots where no sled had passed for days. But Bronson, driven by he knew not what sense of intellectual outrage, by what inherent instinct to fight to the death for a principle, floundered on through the dusk and the moonlight, falling and sobbing now and again, but not for a moment contemplating a return to Cheshire.

It was midnight when he climbed Spindle Hill, a tiny black shadow moving slowly under the waning moon. He pounded on the farmhouse door, until his father's startled voice demanded his name and business. Then he wept with mingled gladness and grief.

They heard his story, shivering before the hastily rekindled fire. When he had finished, his father said, "A flimsy excuse to get home to your mother. You can take your choice, — go back to Cheshire to-morrow or go down to Waterbury and enter Seth Thomas' clock factory."

"I 'll go to the clock factory," said Bronson quickly.

His father sighed as if in disappointment and returned to his bed, but his mother, giving her boy his supper, listened to the repeated explanation and said at last, "If you don't let it stop your education, Bronson, I shall not object, but you 've closed a gate behind you. You must find another for yourself and open it."

"Yes, Mother, I will," said Bronson obediently, and he stumbled off to bed.

And so, the clock factory. The quiet, thoughtful child at work all day, fitting parts of clock works and putting them together, found nothing disagreeable in the work itself. He was not lazy and he had a decided interest in mechanics but in his uncouth surroundings he was lonely and out of place. This sort of work required of him made no demands on his brain, and by carrying one of his precious borrowed books always with him, he did not stagnate, though at the time he thought he did and was terribly unhappy. Yet, rather than go back to Cheshire, he clung to the factory for nearly two years. His father was chagrined and disappointed. His mother, watching him start off each morning along the lonely and precipitous pathway that led the two miles from the farm to the factory, yearned over him, wondered at his gentle obstinacy, worried over him, but never, evidently, lost her faith or understanding. Long years after Bronson wrote of this time to her. It was after Louisa and Anna were born.

In this new relation of father, I seem to be living out my own father's life : in my children I seem to see myself as a child, fondly delighting in his and your approval. My children, calling for their mother, recall the time when I was wont to come to you with that beautiful name on my lips, —

sure of your smiling on me and taking me to your heart. And when my children need correction, then I think of my father's earnest manner with me as I stood before him conscience-stricken and acknowledging my fault. . . . You are associated in my heart with kindness, forbearance long, sympathy with me ever. For when others wronged me it was grateful to have your encouraging look, your approving word. You helped me when I needed help, were glad at any success of mine, never frowned on me when I failed. . . . Preachers I have had, teachers a few, trials and vicissitudes. I have failed in much. I have been schooled into resignation by all. You know all this, when in my ill health and despondence I seemed useless, insignificant in the world. Yet no preaching, teaching or trial or despondence brought me more abundant benefit, none such abiding joy as the recollection of your affectionate encouragement while my character was forming. I pray that my own life never may disgrace yours, and that while cherishing my children I may exercise those graces which were called forth first by your parental solicitude and pains, unrequited.

Much hard thinking went on in that mature boyish mind during the two years of factory work. A great deal of it was about education, the education of young children. He evolved a new spelling book and a new reader, laboriously written out on scraps of paper, in his little room under the eaves after the factory day was finished. He thought much, too, about religion and decided that he would become an Episcopalian.

He undoubtedly was influenced in this decision by the arrival in the neighborhood of the Reverend Mr. Keyes, who established an Episcopal church at Spindle Hill, in the Spindle Hill schoolhouse. Bronson was confirmed and became a lay reader in the little church. It was after this that he asked permission to leave the factory.

Standing before his father that gay Sunday morning in September, Bronson was no longer the confused little boy who had defied, though ever so gently, his clergyman uncle. He was a tall youth now, of nearly sixteen, as tall as his father, well muscled, with a good quality of humor in his lips to offset the seriousness of his blue eyes.

"Father, I'd like your permission to leave the factory."

His father was brushing his clothes preparatory to driving to the meetinghouse.

"You want to go back to Cheshire, son? I don't see how we can spare your wages now."

Bronson shook his head. "I will work here on the farm and go every day for a couple of hours to Mr. Keyes. He will teach me Latin and mathematics."

"Latin and mathematics! Bronson, what are you trying to make of yourself?" This, impatiently, from the boy's father.

"I am going to be a teacher," replied Bronson.

"A teacher! You will starve to death! Though, perhaps you plan to go to college — that would be a wise plan. But Bronson, I can't spare either your time or the money to let you go there. You have a natural skill at farming. Why not be content to settle down here? There's a living here for all of us."

Bronson shook his blond head. "I have to teach. I have to teach little children. They're the only ones that count. I'll give you a full day's time on the farm if you will let me quit the factory, Father."

Mrs. Alcott had come out, dressed for church. She looked from husband to son, then spoke in Bronson's own quiet manner. "Let him have his way, Father."

The father looked in turn from wife to son, the

two of them so curiously alike, then shrugged his shoulders. "Let him have his way, but I warn you he will starve!"

And so the next step was taken, and for a year Bronson sweated by day in field and furrow and pored at night over the books with which Parson Keyes was able to supply him. He was making real progress, he felt, but even this much of education could not be permitted to him. His father needed whatever money the boy could earn, and Bronson, understanding the bitter necessities of the family, acquiesced. But nothing could induce him to return to the clock factory. No! He knew of certain young men who were in the habit of going south in the winter to teach the children of planters. Now, all his quiet, misunderstood life, Bronson was possessed by a deep-seated wanderlust. That desire for change and adventure flared up in him in this emergency. Denied college, denied even the chance to educate himself, he would at least make an adventure of his deprivations and incidentally try out his beloved theories of education. Bronson would go south and teach for the winter.

His family was appalled. "What! Go six hundred miles away from home to earn a few dollars

that you could earn as easy in the clock factory!"
cried his father.

Even his mother was startled. "Bronson, you
have no clothes, no money for the trip."

"I've bargained with that Hessian tailor in Wolcott to trade my fiddle for making me up a suit
of our homespun," replied Bronson.

"Your fiddle! Bronson!"

Bronson nodded, with a sudden flush of tears to
his eyes. His fiddle was very dear to him. He
had made it himself from the bole of a maple tree
that grew in a bilberry tangle, a spot that had
always enchanted him by its quiet beauty and
where he had spent many a magic hour with his
"Pilgrim's Progress." Fashioned from the maple
tree, by means of his knife and the finger skill he
had inherited from his father, he had walked to
New Haven and back to buy the varnish, strings
and resin for completing it and had taught himself
to draw real music from it.

Both father and mother stared at him. Nothing
could have made them understand Bronson's
earnestness about this trip as did the fact that he
had arranged to part with his beloved fiddle to
help bring it about. And then, added Bronson,
"You owe two hundred dollars, Father. You

have no other way to accumulate that great sum other than by the cultivation of this farm, and times are extremely dull. In eight or nine months away I know I can earn half that amount. I'll find a school in the country, near Norfolk. I know I can, and I'll send you home all that I earn outside my board."

An enormous venture and adventure for a country boy of those days. But with his curious, gentle persistence, Bronson put it through. With a little tin trunk that contained all his possessions he started for Norfolk, Virginia. Amos Bronson Alcott, seventeen years old, despite the ugly Hessian suit already in appearance the scholar type, already the young schoolmaster, despite the finely muscled shoulders and the loss of the fiddle, Bronson Alcott, failure and very great gentleman.

He tramped the twenty-five miles to New Haven and there boarded the sloop *Three Sisters*, for Norfolk. He had no money for his passage — eight dollars — but something about Bronson, that charm which every one who knew him, high and low, old and young, records, had its effect on Captain Sperry, and he agreed to give Bronson passage, trusting the young man to pay him later. It was fall and the young scholar-farmer found the long stormy voyage cold and uncomfortable. But he arrived at Norfolk cheerful, though penniless, and at once landed a temporary job as an accountant. This enabled him to pay his bill to the trusting Captain Sperry before the *Three Sisters* started north with her return cargo. He also heard while working on his accounts of a school about twenty miles north of Norfolk where he might get a position.

And so, the red roads of Virginia, the tin trunk and the homespun Hessian suit. He passed some beautiful plantations, he passed an edge of the Dismal Swamp, he passed negro cabins and huts of the poor white trash, feeling moment by moment more bewildered at the strangeness of the country. But he went on steadily to the little town of Kempsville and made application to the school board for a position in the common school. The chairman of the board looked at the certificate with which Bronson's uncle had supplied him, then he looked at Bronson. "This is a man's job, sah," he said to Bronson. "You are too young and green, sah. We need the good juniper club, sah, and an arm that can yield it."

Bronson's eyes twinkled, while he looked from the flabby Southerner to his own finely muscled arm and shoulder. But there was no fooling this Southern politician. He shook his head. There was a gentleness in Bronson's face that belied the forthrightness of his muscles. Nor was there any moving him from his decision.

It was Bronson's first rebuff as a schoolmaster and he took it hard. His prospective profession was very dear to him. He started back to Norfolk, profoundly depressed. Along the edge of the Dismal Swamp a terrible storm overtook him and after battling with it for a time, he finally crouched on his trunk, waiting for the frightful downpour of rain to cease. Sitting thus, with head bowed to the storm, he did not observe the approach of three men until one of them jerked him to his feet and held him while the others emptied his trunk and his pockets. They took his shoes and his hat and left him standing beside his empty trunk, disheveled and breathless. He had put up a tremendous fight but the odds against him had been too great.

He was angry now — angry not only at Virginia but at life, and after a moment's contemplation of the trunk he shoved it into the mouth of the swamp, and started back through the red mud to Norfolk.

38

There was no hope of teaching now, with his meager equipment gone. Bronson reached Norfolk late at night, slept on the wharf, borrowed a pair of shoes from a sailor, and after a talk with a chance acquaintance, a Yankee peddler, he went back to Tisdale, the tin man whose accounts he had been keeping and went to work in his shop. When he had accumulated a small sum of money he bought a supply of almanacs and began his career as a peddler. Each almanac cost him threepence and was sold for ninepence. During the Christmas season his trade was brisk, but it ended with the holidays. Whereupon, young Bronson went to a peddlers' supply merchant and procured credit for about three hundred dollars' worth of goods, trinkets and silks. He packed these goods into two small hand trunks and once more he started out over the red hills of Virginia.

His journal of these days is really an account book of expenditures and earning, but one or two letters north are illuminating.

I am sure it would please you to travel here in Virginia. Hospitality is a distinguishing trait of the people, rich or poor. And the polished manners and agreeable conversations ingratiate the traveler at once in their favor. The planters in

this section are largely an educated class — gentlemen in the best sense of the word. I pass many
an evening at these hospitable homes. It is a
school of manners next to traveling abroad. A
rainy day, too forbidding for travel, offers agreeable entertainment as it gives access to the
planters' libraries which are often voluminous
and attractive. Lanter's Physiognomy, Locke's
Treatise on the Human Understanding, now and
then a novel or biography. — Among the wealthy
and distinguished planters at whose mansions I
have visited — Tabbs, Taliaferros, Nelsons and
Dabreys living on the shores of York and North
Rivers.

The first experience at peddling was of stupendous import to Bronson. For the first time in his
life he actually saw the gentle form of living for
which his soul yearned. He received wonderful
treatment from these Southerners who evidently
recognized at once that here was no common clay,
but a youngster of their own class and predilections.
They made much of him and Bronson absorbed
their polish and manners like a sponge.

When he returned to Spindle Hill in the spring,
he brought with him not only eighty dollars in
cash for his father, but an outward polish of manner that all the ridicule of his family and friends

could not cause him to drop. He worked hard all that summer on the farm, returned to Virginia in the fall, and the following spring he brought his father a hundred dollars. But his father shook his head. There was a gayety and a touch of the cavalier about young Bronson now that his Puritan father did not like. And he had begun to call on the girls of Spindle Hill and Wolcott, which bothered his mother!

But in spite of protests, Bronson started on a third peddling season in the south. This time he went to South Carolina, where he had unbelievably hard luck, ending in his walking across South Carolina and North Carolina to Norfolk! Here, after a few good months of peddling, he was smitten with typhus fever and nearly died. When he finally started homeward he was in debt. But, behold, the terrible influence of the best Virginia families! Instead of paying his debts, he paused in New York to buy clothing, and when he reached Spindle Hill he was clad as no dandy even from Yale ever had been seen either on Spindle Hill or in Wolcott! A tall white hat, a velvet vest, a fine blue broadcloth coat with brass buttons and nankeen trousers strapped over boots so tight that his feet were in torture, a brooch in the frills of his linen shirt, a cane in his well-gloved hand. This was Bronson! — Amos Bronson Alcott, aged twenty, the scholar-peddler gone amuck, to the horror of his family and the overwhelming excitement and admiration of every maiden within the radius of twenty miles.

Ah, well, youth will be paid! What would you have, with all his starving for beauty and all his toil and his thwarted dreams! Let him have his summer with the girls! And he did, like any gay young raking blade.

Then, despite all that his family could say to him, he started back for Virginia in the fall, still with his word and manner of the Southern gentleman upon him. It required two seasons of crushing failure in peddling in the south, followed by a month's sojourn with the Quakers living in Chowan County, Virginia, to bring him back to Puritanism.

His journal recounts failure after failure, with no details except that among the Friends he has read, "No Cross, No Crown", "Barclay's Apology", William Law's "Devout Call", and that he is very ill of ague among these people.

Lying thus ill among these gentle people so fundamentally akin to his own deeper nature, the gay young blade had long hours of suffering and of thought. All the youth in him, all the love of beauty, of women, of luxury, that is an inherent part of youth, especially of that intense and passionate type whose reverse side is Puritan, all the cavalier side of him cried out to him to remain in Virginia, where he had every opportunity to lead the life of a planter. For there were not a few daughters of these fine plantations who would have been glad to marry the charming, penniless young Northerner.

But, battling on the side of the school child of the future, was all the wholesome austerity of his boyhood training, his father's stern Puritanism, his mother's clarity of vision, and that deep-seated desire to give form and birth to his ideal which is the hall-mark of the artistic temperament.

In after years, Bronson said that he was afflicted with shame over his two years of "profligacy." I doubt that. I don't like to feel that Bronson, with his clear vision, tainted the solitary playtime of his life, to whatever lengths it took him, by any sense of shame. God knows, he had a right to his play. I like to believe that, having played and paid, Bronson closed the door on his youth quite deliberately, answered the higher voice, "Yes,

Lord, Thy servant heareth," and took up the heavy burden of his hungry soul again.

He left Virginia in May on foot, with eight and a half dollars in his pocket, and walked all the way to Spindle Hill, arriving there in July — worn, sallow, and tattered, but a man. His youth was buried in the Virginia hills.

Amos Bronson Alcott, aged twenty-two, purged, disciplined, and by the grace of God equipped for his great task. How great a task, only Bronson himself at that time knew. And only a few tremendous souls were to know in the hundred years that followed Bronson's arrival at Spindle Hill, in 1822.

A century ahead of his time. Yet, thanks to Elizabeth Peabody, mother of the American kindergarten, and thanks to his own much-ridiculed habit of keeping endless and meticulously detailed journals, there lies in that quiet library in Concord under the care of "Demi's" wife, the record of ideas and thoughts on education of children that, if America would draw on it, would save America's soul alive to-day, would stay the moral debacle that threatens our children's children.

CHAPTER III

He Discovers Himself

BRONSON turned abruptly from peddling and gay-blading-it in Virginia to school teaching in Connecticut. And the astounding aspect to this is that he taught, not as a novice or as an apprentice to old methods. He taught as one with authority by methods at that time unknown.

How did it happen? Pestalozzi, the great Swiss educational reformer, died about the time Bronson began teaching. It is extremely doubtful if Bronson at this time had read any of Pestalozzi's works. And even if he had, Bronson's method was by no means that of the noted Swiss. Froebel, the inventor of the kindergarten, did not produce his great book on child training until 1826. Bronson never had heard of Froebel at this time. Even if he had, Bronson's system would show no signs of Froebel's influence.

Yet, an observer said in the *Boston Recorder* in 1827, "There is one school of an improved kind, Mr. A. B. Alcott's — the best common school in this state, perhaps in the United States."

And Mr. Samuel May, a Connecticut clergyman, wrote in his journal at this time:

I wrote Mr. Alcott, begging him to send me a detailed statement of his principles and methods in training children. In due time came to me a full account of the school at Cheshire, which revealed such a depth of insight into the nature of man, such a true sympathy with children, such profound appreciation of the work of education, and was withal, so philosophically arranged and exquisitely written that I at once felt assured the man must be a genius and I must know him more intimately. So I wrote inviting him most urgently to visit me.

He came and passed a week with me before the end of the summer. I have never, but in one instance, been so immediately taken possession of by any man I ever met in life. He seemed to me like a born sage and saint. He was a radical in all matters of reform: went to the root of all theories, especially the subjects of education, mental and moral culture.

How did this farm lad, obscure, apparently without education, spring suddenly from obscurity into a brilliant exposition of what was then an extraordinary type of education?

We do not know. All that we do know is that after he returned for the last time from Virginia, Bronson taught for a few months in two or three different country schools and then procured the common school at Cheshire at a salary of twenty-seven dollars a month.

The schoolhouse at Cheshire was the usual box affair of one room, ugly, badly scarred. Bronson knew better than to ask the people of Cheshire for means with which to beautify the schoolhouse. He'd spent his life among these folk and knew them. He went at the job of beautifying by himself. He scraped and painted and cleaned, hung some engravings on the walls, put up a bookshelf on which he arranged his own handful of books — the beginning of the first free library in New England and opened to the children.

They came, suspicious of innovation as were their parents, without the least understanding of a schoolmaster who displayed no birch rod, who was himself beautiful to look upon, and who greeted them with a not-to-be-understood courtesy and affection. To this last they warmed immediately. Bronson's extraordinary charm, coupled with his Virginia manner, would win any child.

The books on the bookshelf excited enormous interest. And when it was found that the books not only could be read in school hours but taken home, Bronson was swamped by requests for the loan of the volumes. Will you kindly note the type of book for which these children were stampeding? Besides several textbooks on reading, spelling and arithmetic, there were stories by Maria Edgeworth, "Pilgrim's Progress", Adam Smith's "Theory of Moral Sentiments", Locke on "The Human Understanding", Cogan's "Treatise on the Passions", and Browne's "Philosophy of the Human Mind!"

Wisely, Bronson began with the old plan of instruction, adding only indoor gymnastics, and the interpretation of little fables by pantomimes. But even these two innovations almost turned the village upside down. Finally, it was decided that these things, though a waste of time, were harmless, and the town settled back to its slumbers. Then, as imperceptibly as he could, Bronson began to substitute the habit of reasoning for that of learning by rote, an absolutely revolutionary idea. He wrote a letter at this time describing his method. In reading it, keep in mind the fact that in the schools of that period there was no method known save that of learning by heart the contents of the scanty textbooks.

I find that whatever children do themselves is theirs, and besides the intellectual progress, this also gives an increase of intellectual power. Originality, at the same time that it marks progress, tends to produce strength and ability to handle more severe trials. *I place much dependence on the practice of analysis in every study.* To define all the words in reading, writing, grammar and geography, as well as in the spelling lesson, is our constant practice. The number of pages gone over is not so much considered as completeness of attainment. But variety is also consulted in the plan of study and fatigue as much as possible avoided. I find that the system that does not cultivate the affections is very imperfect for no permanent results could be had otherwise. Constant, uniform kindness is my most successful instrument.

Not to know columns of words and figures by heart! Not to be able to recite pages of the "American Preceptor"! The village gave Bronson a few months' start, then they roused and took after him, full cry. Twenty-seven dollars a month

49

of their good money for talking and playing with their children, for listening to their children's ideas about God and farming and flowers and death and the soul! Twenty-seven dollars, mind you!

They gossiped about him in the church. They stared at him as though he were a demon man from Mars and not one of their neighbors, who knew their children's needs and potentialities as they could not. They talked of reducing his salary. Bronson allowed them to cut it to twenty dollars a month, — this after he had spent a hundred and twenty dollars of his own money on books and beautifying the school. They demanded of him in committee meetings, "What in tarnation he was trying to do?"

In reply he repeated to them some of the things he said daily to their children :

"It is not from books entirely that our instruction should be drawn. . . . Ideas when recorded in books carry with them a kind of dignity and certainty which awe many into implicit belief. Books often impose the most irrational and absurd conclusions on the peaceful understanding. Millions of minds are in this state of slavery. How shall they escape? . . . Rebel, think for yourselves, let others grumble. Dare to be singular

STEPHENS COLLEGE
LIBRARY

— let others deride. Follow reason; let others dwell in the land of enchantment. Be men: let others prattle. Practice: let others profess. Act: let others sleep. Whatever thy hand findeth to do, that do with all thy might and let a gainsaying, calumniating world speculate on thy proceedings. Let others spend their money for that which is not bread."

Heresy! The whole village was in turmoil. The situation was serious. The children loved their school and were in a state of defiant enthusiasm over Bronson. While the grown-ups were staring at him as he crossed the green, as something unsafe and fearful, the children clung to his coat tails, rode on his shoulders, played at tag with him, and he had a pet name or a term of endearment for each one of them, made quaint little jokes with them.

The Cheshire Academy had been closed for some time, but now, roused by the menace of Bronson's school, the Episcopal clergymen of Connecticut who controlled the academy decided to reopen it. A private school was begun by the local parson. And Bronson began to lose his first fight. Toward the end of his second year, his school dwindled to practically nothing. His diary says:

51

I am the center of all this commotion of feeling. Were I out of the way I think it would subside. I am unable to make more sacrifices. I cannot contend always against avarice and ingratitude. Had I not better leave Cheshire at this time? I do not mean to be hasty or to take any premature step. In pecuniary matters I have laid up little. My wages have been expended on the school in one way or another and I have but a hundred and fifty dollars to show for nearly two years' work.

And so, when he once more was brought before the committee men as a high-handed iconoclast, Bronson resigned. Bronson's feelings as he left the group of men who had turned thumbs down for him were mingled of pride, for his school had attracted fine comment from Mr. Samuel May and other people of culture, and of sadness, for his splendid experiment would seem to have failed at its source — with the people for whom it had been carried on.

As he left the school, however, and started across the green, something happened to him that was to be a solace during all his frustrated years. It was a fine afternoon late in June. The elm-shadowed green was dotted with children at play. But when Bronson appeared under the trees, the youngsters made for him. They had heard the talk among their elders that Bronson was to be sent away. Most of them had been taken from his school before this. Yet he still had been in the village and always accessible to them. And now they stormed him, a good two dozen of them.

"Yes," he answered their queries, "I am going away, my dears."

A howl went up. "Take us with you! We love you! I never knew I had a brain till I went to your school. We'll never forget you! Come back to us! Oh, come back!"

And then a little girl whose arms were filled with cowslips rushed up to Bronson and filled his pockets and the brim of his hat with the gay yellow blossoms. Another child rushed for lilacs and another for syringas and Bronson, laughing as they pursued him, reached his boarding place crowned with flowers and followed to the very door by the blessings and the tears of the children of Cheshire.

So the school failed and Cheshire went happily back to the methods that it had used for over a hundred years.

After he left Cheshire, Bronson worked on the farm for a while. It was haying season and all hands were needed. Then he went to visit Rev.

53

Samuel May at Brooklyn, Connecticut. There he met Abba May. She was a very tall young woman of magnificent physique, flashing dark eyes, a sweet, sensitive mouth, and masses of waving dark chestnut hair. It was a case of love at first sight between these two, and through all the vicissitudes of their long life together, they remained passionate lovers. They were remarkable foils for each other. Abba, high-tempered, quick of tongue, witty, a bit sharp, free-handed, intelligent rather than intellectual, a man's kind of woman. Bronson, serene, without repartee but probably the greatest conversationalist this country ever will know, humorous and fun-loving but not witty, a generous rather than an impulsive giver, an intellectual giant.

Abba's ideas about herself were neither ornate nor enthusiastic. She wrote, late in life, an autobiography which is a model of modesty and brevity.

I was born October 8, 1800, christened at King's Chapel by Rev. Dr. James Freeman, and named for my grandmother, Abigail May. My father was Col. Joseph May, my mother Dorothy Sewall and I was the youngest of twelve children. Born sickly and nursed by a sickly woman, I have survived all my family. My schooling was much interrupted by ill health, but I danced well and at the dancing school (1812–1814) remember having for partners some boys who afterwards became eminent divines. I did not love study but books were always attractive.

In 1819 I went to pass a year with Miss Allyn of Duxbury (daughter of Rev. Dr. Allyn, the parish minister) who assisted me in reviewing my studies: and with her, I studied French, Latin, botany, read history extensively, and made notes on many books such as Hume, Gibbon, Hallam's Middle Ages, Robertson's Charles V., etc.

In October, 1825, my mother died. In 1827, while at my brother's in Brooklyn, I met Mr. Alcott, whose views on education were very attractive. I was charmed by his modesty, his earnest desire to promote better advantages for the young. Not an educated man himself, he was determined that the large funds of Connecticut ($1,000,000) for educational purposes should be used for higher ends than was the case at that time. The same year, Dr. Joseph Tuckerman with Mrs. Minot, Miss Cabot (afterward Mrs. Foller) my sister Grace and others suggested an infants' school in Boston. Mr. Alcott was sent for, to organize such a school. This brought him to Boston and I had further opportunities of becoming acquainted with him.

After her meeting with Bronson, she evidently felt that her history was indistinguishable from his, for at this point, the account ceases. They saw each other but a short time at this first meeting but long enough to prepare ground for the quaint correspondence which they carried on for several years following.

Bronson got a position as district teacher in Bristol, Connecticut, in 1827-1828. He started with sixty pupils and his salary was twenty-three dollars a month. He began with high hopes, of course, but was not so sanguine of the backing of parents as he had been in the early days of Cheshire. The most noteworthy fact about his experience at Bristol was not that it failed, but that he set those experiences down on paper, using, you will observe, the editorial "we."

Jan. 10, 1828. A happy state of feeling pervades our little community at the schoolhouse: they are interested and happy. The work of regeneration in their hearts has commenced and had we time and the control of them in all their concerns, we are sure to effect all that theologians attribute to the word Regeneration. But we are not permitted to do this: prejudices, strong and inveterate assail us on all sides: there are only two or three grown persons with whom we can freely converse and our opinions fully developed would alarm people. Hence a course of prudent compromise is the only hope of success. . . .

Jan. 14. The determination seems active with a few that we shall not succeed or in other words that their children shall not learn by regular attendance at the schoolroom. It cannot be expected that those who estimate progress in their children by the readiness with which they can spell long columns of words, of whose meaning they know nothing, should approve our plan or estimate our labor of much worth; for in these things we do nothing, nor do we intend to waste our time in the useless, the positively stupefying process of covering long words from a spelling book or in committing and reciting rules and sentences of which they know nothing.

Jan. 24. The influence of kindness with which the young under my care are treated, begins to show itself in their manners. These affections are in a good state, — I know not how long an envious, gainsaying world will permit me to pursue the familiar, affectionate manner in which I have recently treated the scholars. Already it has become a subject of discussion among their parents : — they know not what to think of treating children in so kind a manner.

February 1. For the last ten days the school

has been visited by several persons of the district, all of whom have expressed their approbation of our plan, leaving the school with impressions more favorable than they had entertained. . . . It is some satisfaction to find our plans becoming subject of discussion and attracting notice about. Anything to agitate still water and perhaps the maxim may here be well equipped.

February 4. Those dissatisfied with our plans have engaged an instructor and commenced another school this day with fifteen pupils.

Feb. 17. My moral opinions are subjects of discussion among those who are bound to the faith of antiquity and determined to support it at all events. The clergyman here in a recent discourse alluded to my opinions, attempted to controvert them and to establish what he called the truth. I cannot bring these men to discuss the points in question with me. They seem unwilling to bring them forward except among their own party. *Until the Christian system is brought directly into the details of family and school government, the world must blunder along as it has in all preceding ages.*

Mar. 28. Our term of five months this day expired. I closed the school, with regret. . . .

But he was twenty-nine now and beginning to see his future clearly. His regret was not discouragement.

CHAPTER IV

The Lovers

DURING the short term in Bristol, the correspondence with Abba May throve amazingly. It is my impression that Abba was a bit forward in urging the young schoolmaster to write often: at least she did not show the extreme reticence that the best literature of the day pictures as inseparable from a young lady's deportment toward the brutal sex!

In the early days of 1828 she wrote to him at Bristol as follows:

Your letter to my brother was handed to us by the laughing doctor a few hours after Mr. May's departure. We had swept the hearth, closed the shutters and determined to be happy though the center of light and heat had departed from our home. Your letter cheered us much. And do let us often be cheered during this inclement weather by your word and spirit. I promised to say something on the subject of your former letters: but, my good friend, how can I when you

59

have said all, and so well? The maternal orbit so beautifully described, — infantile development so happily exposed, — the moral constitution of God's Providence so firmly supporting the whole scheme, — I can only subscribe myself a realist in your theory.

I fervently hope that your labors will be appreciated in Bristol and your success commensurate with your exertions. If prejudice tinctures opinion there as it does here, you may toil seven years, yea, seventy times seven — and not establish truth. My poor brother has spent six of his best years in this place and has accomplished little. . . . My brother would persuade me that I lack charity. I confess my cloak is not so large as his nor so well lined.

You inquire about my reading. I have read Locke, Stewart, Browne, — the latter twice. But my reading for the last few years has been rather desultory. My health has been so variable and domestic trials have at times so oppressed my mind that I have been guided by the taste of the moment as to the choice of a book. We are at present reading Napoleon by Scott. Dr. Channing has reviewed it in his masterly style. He makes Napoleon's greatness to consist in Action which is his third grade of greatness. His first is moral, his second intellectual. Washington he ranks the greatest because he is a moral man; he

served no selfish ends and though he made no high-
roads over the Alps, yet he climbed the mount and
saw the Promised Land.

Pray write me often and if my letters are not too
careless and stupid, I shall be satisfied to keep up
this form of friendship: for forms, you know, are
the limbs of friendship, though not its life. And
now, my friend, snuff the candle and pick out the
subject matter of this letter if you can.

Bronson, immersed in the double difficulty of
formulating his theories of child training and of
warding off parental interference with his pupils,
did not respond with the fullness that his biogra-
pher might wish. He merely noted in his diary
on the day he received Abba's letter: "Received
a communication of an interesting nature from
Brooklyn."

But when he turned the key on his Bristol failure,
he did not, as had been his wont, go to his mother
for sympathy. He went to Brooklyn. Abba,
who was by this time deeply in love with Bronson,
had some difficulty in concealing her feeling for
this tired-eyed young man. But the dignity and
aloofness of his manner steadied her and she
turned the desire to comfort him into practical
suggestions for his next move. Bronson, who had

wondered vaguely why he had turned to Brooklyn
rather than to Spindle Hill, listened to her plans
and told himself that as of old, his man's instinct
had led him to the Sibyl for advice. The result
of the three days' talk with Abba, now before the
fire in the minister's study, now in the kitchen with
Bronson wiping the dishes, now in the woods,
where the pussy willows were hanging out their
little pelts, was that Bronson used his meager sav-
ing in a trip to Philadelphia and Boston, there to
study the possibilities for starting infant schools.
And Abba did not let her desire to help rest
there. She was, during the spring, offered a position as teacher of a little charity school in Boston.
She at once saw here an opportunity for Bronson
and in June Bronson found himself established as
master of the school, with a free hand for his educational experiments and with the prospect, if the
school grew, of Abba's being employed as his assistant. His heart overflowed with gratitude. And
she was beautiful. How could he have failed to
warm to the thought of her working with him?

Abba was in Boston, when he reached there,
and he made the following entry in his diary:

June 1, 1828. In the afternoon, visited Miss
May in relation to the infant school for which she

has applied as assistant teacher. I am unwilling she should thus engage with the hope of continuing it when I leave, for I am desirous that she should assist in the more desirable situation which I propose in a school of a higher order. . . . But perhaps this is indulging a hope which we can never realize. In the acquisition of this lady as an assistant, I think we should obtain that kind of help which is indispensable — I know of no young lady equally intelligent on the subject of education and no one feeling a deeper interest in the welfare of the young.

But Abba's brother Samuel objected to her acting as Bronson's assistant. He said that it would breed gossip. Abba was too handsome, Bronson too much liked by women to make such an alliance feasible. So Abba wrote rather mournfully to Bronson, in July:

We meet so seldom and our conversation is necessarily so desultory that I must be excused for venturing to visit you occasionally this way: more particularly when I have anything to suggest for the furtherance of your "prospective plans." I have relinquished the idea of ever undertaking anything of this kind in Boston. . . . You wish I believe, some lady to be associated with you in your Infant School, which I understand is to consist of boys only. Will you allow me to rec-

THE FATHER OF LITTLE WOMEN

ommend a lady in every way qualified for this sacred trust? A Miss Savage, of Salem, the author of "James Talbot", "The Factory Girl", etc.

She is not engaged at present in any publication. She maintains herself by her needle and her health suffers for engagements more congenial to her active, fertile brain. . . . I am going to the country for a few days and shall see an intimate friend of hers who can ascertain her mind on the subject, if you would like to have me propose it. Her age is about forty. She is sedate without austerity, cheerful without levity, and has perfect control of her temper and feelings. I wish you to treat me candidly. If you have any other modifications of your plan, don't hesitate to set aside my proposition. . . . May I hope to hear from you this week as I shall probably go to Hingham or Brookline the next? If visiting is incompatible with your engagements, do not hesitate to place your thoughts on paper. They are particularly valuable to me in this form, as they in some degree become my own.

Bronson, reading this letter, experienced a decided feeling of disappointment and chagrin. Miss May, he told himself, was the only woman he knew who shared his ideals of teaching. It was not kind or fair of her to lead him to take the school in the expectation that she would help him, then to desert him without explanation. Miss Savage, indeed ! — "cheerful without levity, sedate without austerity." He thought of Abba's brilliant, laughing eyes, her love of dancing, her quick, gay manner, her stinging temper. What a companion she was ! And she was trying to foist the author of insipid "James Talbot" on him ! It was a month before he could bring himself to write Abba in the decorous manner becoming to a schoolmaster.

You will place me under still deeper obligations by mentioning my proposed school to your friend, Miss Savage, and ascertaining her views about it. Certainly I should esteem myself fortunate in receiving the assistance of so accomplished a lady. But must I relinquish the pleasing anticipation awakened a year since while visiting in Brooklyn, of *your* assistance ? I must acquiesce if your decision is irrevocable. But I shall hope that you still will sometimes visit my little circle in Salem Street. I thought I caught a glimpse of you in that vicinity the other day. Shall I add that only my diffidence prevented me from accosting you then ?

Abba did not reply to this tardy acknowledgment of her gesture. She was trying to find a satisfactory position at teaching and sedulously avoiding Salem Street. Bronson found that he was giving many precious moments that should have been given to his school experiments, to wondering how he had offended Miss May. So one day in August, he devoted a portion of his infinitesimal salary to the purchase of a ruffled shirt and a new satin stock and went to take his friend to task.

He found her in company with half a dozen other boarders in a stuffy little parlor and immediately invited her for a walk on the Common. Abba was leaving the next day for a visit in Hingham and she told Bronson that she had quite reconciled herself to dropping out of his life. They were passing under the drooping branches of a great elm as she spoke and Bronson was swept by one of the few uncontrollable impulses of his life. He suddenly caught her hands, drew her into the shadows and took her to his heart. He felt quite mad and told her so. Then, as he laid his lips to hers, all power of coherent thought left him.

That night Abba wrote to Samuel:

My dear brother — I should have answered your kind letter before, but ever since I wrote you last my mind and heart have been on the rack. I am engaged to Mr. Alcott, not in a school, but in the solemn, the momentous capacity of friend and wife. He has been attached to me since the evening of our conversation in Brooklyn, but circumstances have prevented the disclosure of his feelings. I found it remained for me to dissolve all communion with him or give him that encouragement and promise that should secure to him my future interest. The former I could not do. I found myself clinging to his interests, distressed by his long absences. I found on analyzing my regard for him that I loved him. I therefore resolved on the latter conclusion. I do think him in every respect qualified to make me happy. He is moderate. I am impetuous. He is modest and humble. I am forward and arbitrary. He is poor but we both are industrious. Why may we not be happy?

He has made an exposition of his character to me. So simple. So pure. So just what Jesus loved. We talk little of heaven but are already deep in schemes for our future independence and comfort. . . . I am afraid he is embarrassed a little in his circumstances. I feel anxious for his success but still feel the greatest security in his habits of industry and method. I never felt so happy in my life. I feel already an increase of moral energy. I have something to love, to live for. I have felt a loneliness in this world that was making a misanthrope of me in spite of anything I could do to overcome it. I intend now for two years to live a third of my time at home, a third of my time with sister Louisa and a third of my time with you and fit myself to undertake and discharge with cheerfulness and honor the duties of a wife. Help me, my dear Sam, to the accomplishment of all my good resolutions. My heart is as boundless as eternity in its loves and charities. Do write me directly and continue to be to me that sincere, candid friend as you always have been the most tender and affectionate of brothers to

Your sister, Abba.

Her diary continues the story:

Hingham, August 20, — Left Boston at ten o'clock in a little packet for Hingham which we reached at five o'clock and found Mr. Brooks' family expecting us and very hospitably glad to see us. Passed the evening in conversation and retired early; but sleep forsook my eyes and slumber my eyelids. I lived over the preceding evening which had been one of peculiar intense feeling.

Bronson followed her to Hingham the following day.

We spent the day delightfully on the rocks and beach fishing, shelling, getting moss, etc. We had our dinner in a homely style at Mr. Nichols who allows people to make every convenient use of his house but will take no compensation. The day was fine, — ocean and heaven seemed to blend in one expanse of blue. Oh! had I Jubal's lyre or Miriam's tuneful voice, I should breathe praises of Ocean who approached us in solemn swells and retired in solemn dignity, bathing the beach with tears and chanting a requiem in his hollow murmur. The sun, beaming on the waves which ever and anon kissed in this wild emotion, seemed contesting between smiles and tears.

Friday, 22nd. Passed the evening at Tranquillity Grove. What a magic moonlight throws over everything! The most indifferent objects assume a light or shade that gives them interest.

Bronson returned to Boston on Sunday. On Monday, Abba wrote in her diary:

Rather impatient for some intelligence from Boston. I shall write tomorrow if nothing arrives. How much I already enjoy in this connection! I hope I am grateful. . . . *Evening.* Nothing from Boston.

Tuesday morning, 26th. Have a letter from my friend. Exhibited more pleasure than was consistent with my worldly stoicism. The girls laughed and declared there was more fire in my eye and warmth in my cheek than they ever saw before. I retreated to my room. My friend says and reiterates again and again that we will "live to make each other wiser, better, happier." Again "Our lives shall be spent in the elevation and advancement of each other." May our good resolutions be strengthened; may our hearts become sublimated by this union and our minds exalted; our lives humble, our hopes elevated, our purpose, Heaven! I must write, today.

Wednesday, 27th. Wrote to my friend yesterday. I must write with more care for my dictum, chirography, arrangement. I mean to continue this exercise of noting down what I do if nothing else. My friend suggested it when I left home and I will try to continue it agreeably. His success has been so great it adds force to all he recommends. One example is worth ten precepts. I shall return, I hope, in a week, and not leave home again for several months.

This is the letter, dated August 26, 1828:

My dear Friend: — As I approached the desk to thank my friend for his continued proofs of remembrance and affection, I laughingly said to those about me, "Come girls, give me a text for my sermon." They shouted, "There's nothing true but Heaven." The emotion it excited in my heart soon revealed itself in my eyes. They called me the "crying philosopher." Let them laugh. I am incapable of writing a comment on such a text at this moment for I am fully of the belief there *is* something true on earth and you, beloved friend, are constantly convincing me I am right. I cannot preach on the evanescent joys of life when I feel myself in the full possession of something so very real as I believe our friendship to be. I will believe these girls have never enjoyed this *real* comfort, this sunshine of life. . . .

> "Celestial Happiness, where'er she stoops
> To visit earth, one shrine the goddess finds,
> And one alone, — to make her sweet amends
> For absent Heaven — the bosom of a friend ;
> Where heart meets heart, reciprocally soft,
> Each other's pillow to repose, divine."

Your love taught me there is truth and sound philosophy on earth. The climate is not too cold for truth and love. . . . I do not expect to gather flowers all my life. There is much to wonder at and adore in the rougher formations of nature. I love the trials to which we are exposed. . . .

I shall probably return on Tuesday next. You need make no apologies for your Mss. They are full of entertainment and instruction and were they not it would be a pleasure to read what you think it worth while to write. Am I not zealous ? This may be my sin. You shall correct by all the temperance you see fit to exercise but I love to see zeal in a good cause. And I will apply one of Jeremy Taylor's beautiful illustrations to my case. "So long as the flame kindles and the light shines, so long does the mind of men stand close to the altar and wait upon the sacrifice. The river that runs slow and creeps by the banks, and begs of every turf to let it pass is drawn into little hollownesses and dies with diversion; but when it runs with vigorousness and a full stream it breaks down every obstacle, stays not to be tempted by little avocations, but runs into the sea through full and useful channels."

I am leading you I know not where. I cannot help being impressed with the idea which your letters and conversation invariably leave in my mind that you are a *trembling believer*. You don't doubt me but you *don't realize, etc*. Now this is a spirit you must exorcise. I realize and am in full enjoyment of all which such a reality can afford me. I close by quoting Montaigne, who in trying to describe the affection he felt for his friend, said "When I ask myself whence it is that I feel this joy, this ease, this serenity when I see him, it is because it is *he*, it is because it is *I;* and this is all I can say."

When word of the engagement reached him, Bronson's cousin, Doctor William Alcott, wrote a letter of congratulations and of praise of Bron-

son's character to Abba. When Bronson read
the letter, he wrote in his diary :

Thus the pencil of friendship points. Would
that the original were like the copy, would that the
coloring were not too high ! What he has said I
am, let me be emulous to be. With this for my
standard of imitation and with the influence of the
gentle being with whom I am to spend my days,
what may I not become ? Aid me, Thou God of
Love ! to improve my opportunities, to turn all
the favors of thy grace to the formation of character — to assimilate myself to thee ! Aid her to
be all that Thou and she desire : aid us both in the
progress of life and felicity !

His mother wrote from Spindle Hill :

Affectionate Son, — We received your letter
dated September 5 and read it with much pleasure
and satisfaction. We rejoice and I trust are
thankful for the prosperity of our children — and
particularly for you as you have been a man of
misfortune, — and hope that your prospects will
not raise you so high as to induce you to forget that
you, as well as others, are subject to disappoint-
ments. Every circumstance seems favorable to
all of us. Doctor William says that he is surprised
when he reflects on your prospects a few years since
and your present ones. Your future prosperity
my son, depends upon your future conduct. I

am assured that that will be good. Tell Miss May that I thank her for her friendly letter. I should like to write her; but my poor education and the habit of writing but little must be my reasons for omitting it. I hope to see her one day and communicate my thoughts and feelings to her by conversation. I know you are enjoying life with your friends in Boston, and particularly with her. I hope you have considered well and decided in your own mind concerning your companion for life and from your usual character I have no reason to doubt but what you have. Give my love to your companion and write us when we may have the pleasure and happiness of seeing her and you.

When Bronson showed this letter to Abba it raised in her a fierce regret that her own mother could not know Bronson. She tried to describe her mother to her lover:

My mother's most striking characteristic was her affectionate disposition. She adored her husband and children, she loved the whole human family and went about doing good. Her attachments were strong, her sufferings proportionally severe. She was constantly solicitous that her daughters should be educated as fit companions for man. . . . She never said great things but did ten thousand generous ones . . . her life was a series of kind compliances, virtuous purposes, energetic exertion. She looked well to the ways of her household and ate not the bread of idleness; she opened her mouth with caution and on her tongue was the law of kindness.

Said Bronson of this characterization, "I can in some degree realize the character of this good woman from her effect upon her children. It was this influence that made our Abba, the affectionate friend, the disinterested companion, the ardent lover. It was this that imparted to the original strength of her mind, its energy and independence, to her heart, its delicate sensibilities and firm purposes."

It was very important, this engagement between Abba May and Bronson Alcott, important not only because of the children that were to come from the marriage it prefaced but because Abba's fiery, passionate nature was to have so decided an influence on Bronson's life work. They were engaged for two years before Bronson felt financially justified in marrying: years endured by Bronson with his usual calm and tender philosophy and by Abba with impatient and poignant longing. Bronson had his cherished profession for solace. Abba, called back to Brooklyn, Connecticut, to care for her brother's children, had nothing save housework, which always was and always would be distasteful to her. Her fine mind needed other food than dishwater.

Bronson, absent minded and work-absorbed, neglected her a good deal and she wrote him fiery letters of reproach.

You do not, you cannot love me, my friend, as I do you, else you would fly to quill and paper as your one means of easing this pain of separation. In my daily dreadful grind, I go tear blinded with longing for one word from you, yet day succeeds days, and no word comes. I cannot endure it. Either you must give me all or nothing.

Bronson read the letter in the little schoolroom and groaned aloud. He needed no words to keep his love flaming. It burned steadily, fed, he said, on the essence of his soul.

Says his diary, regretfully :

August 1829. I do not yet give my companion all the sympathy and kindness which her delicate nature requires : could I be with her constantly, I should better understand her sympathies and touch them as they need.

December 19, 1829. Wrote to my companion at Brooklyn. I am apprehensive that my not writing earlier will make her anxious. For unworthy as I am of her love and confidence, the proofs of her disinterested affection have been too often given to leave further room for doubt. I have too often pained her sensibilities by allusions to doubts and fears, — one of those habits of my mind which though necessary in the pursuit of truth, is perhaps questionable in the delicate expression of love where the language of confidence is invariably demanded by the heart. I will try to avoid not only such expressions but the feelings that allow it, — for to the most reasoning woman, a reasoning love is uncongenial and suspicious. Perhaps a woman must trust and find her happiness in this, more than our sex can.

January 25, 1830. Heard from my companion in Brooklyn. Our marriage in the spring seems to me, on the whole, warranted by existing circumstances. Were none but myself involved in the consequences, I should not hesitate a moment. But the happiness of another may be involved by the decision. But are not the ills of life as well as its happinesses, alleviated by united sympathy and affection, and can separation avert their presence? Have I not rather listened to a deceitful delusion when I imagined I was obeying the dictates of reason? Why should we be longer separated in anticipation of distant and dubious evils, when the miseries of absence are the most certain, the most increasing we can feel? Providence bestows his bounties equally upon all and it will be our folly alone if we do not obtain our share.

Bronson knew himself, knew that somehow he would never be quite adequate to the demands Abba would make upon him. But what could he do? How could he be wise for both, for Abba in love was as ardent and as impractical as a child?

And so on the 23d of May, 1830, Abba came up to Boston with Sam and Lucretia, her brother and his wife. And in the lovely spring afternoon, the Reverend Samuel performed the marriage ceremony in King's Chapel. They were a singularly beautiful pair, both of great stature, the man so fair, the woman so richly dark. Bronson had spent a portion of his carefully hoarded funds on a blue broadcloth swallowtail, white nankeen trousers, strapped under the boots, a white bell-shaped beaver, an ivory-headed cane. Abba wore a plaid silk walking dress, with enormous puff sleeves, and a small hoop in the skirt which, in the prevailing mode, was six inches from the floor, showing heelless black sandals and white stockings. Her rich chestnut hair was in curls, a bunch over either ear and another high on the crown of her head. Her hat was a black beaver with a broad brim and a great bow of plaid ribbon to match the frock stood a foot above the crown.

There were very few people to witness the ceremony. Bronson had insisted on this. He was overcoming his bashfulness but had not yet reached the point where he could bear to be stared at "by a heterogeneous crowd during this awful and sacred moment."

They went directly to their rooms on Tremont Street to begin their honeymoon.

CHAPTER V

The Philadelphia Experiment

THERE followed a period of unalloyed happiness for the lovers, Abba so ardent, and Bronson so profoundly moved. It was to Sam's wife, Lucretia, that Abba wrote, shortly after the wedding, the wonder and joy of it.

June 15, 1830. I am delighted, my dear Lu, at the confidential and communicative spirit of your letter. And though I never have really witnessed the beams of the honeymoon, yet there may have been one in the heaven of my married life. Its genial influence may have affected me all this time without my knowing it. I hope we may go through life infected by this lunacy. My husband (hallowed be the name) is all I expected — this is saying a good deal. For in my belief there are few who in the romantic days of courtship and promise do not overlook those essential qualifications so necessary to rational and permanent happiness. Love is and ever has been with us a principle and not a passion, and I have already seen the good effects operating in our lives and conversations.

80

I already feel the influence of moral and intellectual society constantly and exclusively enjoyed. My husband's habits are all the quiet, contemplative kind and I only fear that with my distaste for society in general we shall all be too apt to rest satisfied with our own society in preference to any more extensive and diffusive means of social enjoyment.

He is tranquil and firm, which you know is directly opposite to my constitution so full of emotion and strong prejudices, placable but passionate, my dislikes are antipathies, my prepossessions, loves. How important, with this temperament, that my future companion should be a man of judgment and decision, tranquil and equable. He is all this which gives me hopes that I too may become one day what my friends would wish to have me.

At first Abba worked side by side with Bronson in the school.

The little charity school in Salem Street had served to interest some of the leading minds of Boston in Bronson's revolutionary theories of child training. In the fall of 1828, he had started a school for boys on Common Street, beginning with the children from Boston's first families at a tuition of twenty-eight dollars a year. By April of 1829, he had thirty pupils with a prospect of more. He removed to more convenient quarters in Tremont Street and there he was located when he and Abba were married.

As he worked, day by day, and month by month, putting his theories into practice, he found himself making certain important modifications in his attitude toward the pupils, on the side of discipline. But his ideas on the method of imparting information remained unchanged. He began to write articles for the various journals on education and this brought him into correspondence with men and women in Philadelphia and New York, to whom these theories were as manna to the starving. Philadelphia was at this time more alive than Boston to the need of a change in teaching methods. Robert Haines, a wealthy Quaker, devoted to cattle breeding and natural science, was so excited over Bronson's articles that he visited the Tremont Street school. The result of this was an invitation to Bronson to come to Philadelphia and there, backed by Mr. Haines' money, establish a school after Bronson's own heart.

Abba and Bronson did not hesitate long over accepting the invitation. The Boston school was doing well but the income from it was a decidedly fluctuating quantity. Haines offered a steady salary and delightful surroundings. In December, 1830, they removed to Philadelphia.

Several months were spent in preparations for opening the school which had grown hugely in Haines' mind. It was not to consist of Bronson's work alone. There was to be an upper boys' school presided over by two well-known educators whom it was proposed Bronson should train in his ideas, and a lower school, of both boys and girls. Bronson was to teach the children up to nine years of age, then pass them on to William Russell, editor of the *Journal of Education*, in the upper school.

Bronson's diary gives an excellent picture of Philadelphia as he found it.

Compared with Boston there seems to exist here all the plainness and simplicity of manners for which the city is distinguished. The subjects most cultivated and which conversation generally turns to seem to be the physical sciences; while those most discussed in Boston are the metaphysical and ethical. The influence of the Friends upon conversation, manner and thought is apparent; subjects connected with utility, comfort and practical morals seem most congenial to their minds. Economy and utility, rather than expenditure and taste seem the popular idols: these, however, are frequently united in a style of magnificence where expenditure seems more conspicuous from the unusual plainness into which it is wrought. The wealthy dwell in expensive houses and form an aristocracy of which wealth rather than intelligence is the prominent quality.

It finally was decided to locate the infant school in Germantown. Abba wrote to her father, Colonel May, in Boston, one of her practical, illuminating letters :

Feb. 3, 1831. — We have been engaged for the last few days in making preparations for Germantown. A very good house not far from Friend Haines and near the Academy is now vacant which we can hire for a reasonable sum : and as a few weeks will elapse before the institution commences operations, our friends thought it best for us to secure the situation. Mr. Alcott has had many reasons for vacillating about his decision between city and country : but the former cannot even be tried without greater pecuniary resources, and the latter is secure though less advantageous ultimately. Mr. Haines has been indefatigable in making everything secure, without binding us to any engagement, which we may see cause to regret.

Our prospects are pleasant and encouraging ; we have found many very important friends and though in Germantown shall not be cut off from this generous and intelligent society. We enjoy the simple manners and habits of the people here very much. You would be delighted with the cheerful and natural behavior of the most wealthy and aristocratic part of society. The Friends are the majority and this, I suppose, gives a dignified, tranquil and simple air to the whole.

Thus it will be seen that it was with a not inconsiderable flourish that the Alcotts opened the school in Germantown. For a time all went well. There were many pupils who paid inadequate fees for which Friend Haines paid subsidy. There was a charming home and an adequate number of servants to care for the boarding scholars and for Abba. Abba needed care for on March 19, 1831, a daughter was born to her, Anna Bronson Alcott. The baby was twelve days old when Abba wrote to her brother and sister-in-law of the great event.

March 29, 1831. My dear Sam and Lu, you have rejoiced with me e'er this in the safe birth of my child. Lucretia, I suppose, is ready with her condolence that it is a girl. I don't need it. My happiness in its existence and the perfection of its person is quite as much as I can well bear. Indeed, I cannot conceive that its being a boy could add thereto. She is in good health, perfectly quiet and is a true May for eating and sleeping. Her

85

father has already begun a diary of her progress. Should she be spared to us, it will be highly interesting both to her and ourselves. And should she be taken away, we shall be glad that her early infancy was recorded. And had she not lived an hour after the pangs of birth, I still should rejoice that she had been born. My joy of that moment was sufficient compensation for the anguish of thirty-six hours. But she has lived long enough to open all the fountains of my higher and better nature. She has given love to life and life to love.

The remembrance of that trying period has passed and that most interesting of all occupations begun, the care of my child. And delightful it is. I would not delegate it to an angel. I am at times impatient to dismiss my nurse that not even she should participate with me in this pleasure. I have an excellent nurse, good physician and delightful chamber which for the last ten days has been a heaven to me, or rather a scene of blissful enjoyment, a new creation.

My husband has not left my room many hours since my illness. And although engaged principally at his table with his manuscripts, his presence has shed tranquillity on the scene. He is very happy in the little girl and I predict that his wife has not diminished value for having become mother. He justifies his character well, dear Lu, for domestic and parental excellence, inferior to none.   He is not one of the number who cry Lord! Lord! but he does quietly and faithfully the will of his God.   He does not pay tithe of mint, annice and cummin but attends to the weightier matters of the law — justice, truth, good will to man. . . . I have felt a wish to tell you myself that I am the happy mother of a living child.   If there be any in the world to sympathize in my happiness, surely it is you.   It is a happiness not to be communicated to every one.   All could not understand the sacred, pure emotions that at times overwhelm me.

Excuse my egotism.   If ever selfishness is excusable it is in a moment like this when such new and tender ties are formed, never to be broken.   Ties which age must strengthen and not even death can dissolve.

Kiss my sweet nephew for me and tell him to come and see his little cousin, this summer.   Anna Bronson Alcott is an amiable little bud.   Perhaps she will be a blossom worthy his plucking one of these days.   Farewell.   Write me soon.   For though so happy in my new relations, I am not unmindful of those who were everything to me in the day of celibacy and sorrow.

Your affectionate, Abba.

Stupendous days, these, for the young schoolmaster.   He was, as his wife wrote, of a domestic type and untiring in his devotion to his home and exceedingly skillfull in helping care for the baby. And his fatherhood consecrated him anew to his life work. His school had not opened yet and thus he had time not only to minister to Abba and the baby but to begin some important literary work. He began his "Observations on the Life of Childhood", which for minuteness of detail in the study of an infant probably never has been equaled. Published and in the hands of the modern psychologist it would be classic. He was giving, also, a series of lectures in Philadelphia on his views of education.

Philadelphia must have been considerably riven and rent at this time by philosophical contention. Some one was publishing articles on the theories of Pestalozzi, the Swiss educator and reformer, in the *Register of Pennsylvania*, a weekly newspaper. Bronson had little in common with Pestalozzi but anything that led to discussion of the training of children helped his cause. The large German element in Philadelphia had much interest in discussing Bronson's theories, but no patience with their application in the schoolroom. He was too gentle for them, had not yet developed the fine system of discipline that made his later work successful. The Friends, on the other hand, found

his gentleness a strong asset. But they could n't
be made to see the practical importance of his
theories. Only a very few of them, like Haines,
could bridge the gap between Bronson's schoolroom and life.

But all this writing, discussing and lecturing was
excellent training for the young schoolman. He
was deeply happy and so was Abba. She wrote
on May 7 to her father:

I am glad if the sentiments in my last letter
gratified you. They were the natural expressions
of the full and grateful heart of a mother. My
little girl is now seven weeks old: neither she nor
myself have known sickness since her presence
made my heart glad. She is blessed with her
father's mild and gentle spirit and gives me no
anxiety or trouble. Mr. Alcott has kept a record
of her physical and intellectual progress which is
truly interesting. It seems as if she were conscious of his observations and were desirous of fur-
nishing him daily with an item for his record. Our
arrangements have been completed at last, after
some vacillation from several circumstances. But
Mr. Haines has now bought a fine house for our
department of the school. It is situated on the
main street, the grounds and garden standing
back and including an acre or more, all beautifully
laid out. Our garden is planted, our house

painted, inside and out, and neatly furnished, and we are making arrangements for our children as boarders.

On the 23d of May, Abba wrote a letter to Sam, giving a complete picture of their situation. This was one of the high moments of Abba's difficult married life and she gave it, unconsciously enough, poor dear, full value.

This is the anniversary of my wedding day and I now devote an hour to you in living over the past and projecting the future. It has been an eventful year, — a year of trial, of happiness, of improvement. I can wish no better fate to any sister of the sex than has attended me since my entrance into the conjugal state. Our prospects are good. I wish you could see our delightful situation. You would not wonder that we went to our last dollar to establish ourselves in this little paradise. Imagination never pictured out to me a residence so perfectly to my mind. I wish my friends could see how delightfully I am settled.

My father has never married a daughter or seen a son more completely happy than I am. I have cares and soon they will be arduous ones : but with the mild, constant and affectionate sympathy and aid of my husband, with the increasing health and loveliness of my quiet and bright little Anna, with the coöperation and efficient care of my nurse and housekeeper, a house where neatness and order would cope with Federal Court, a garden lined with raspberries, currants, gooseberry bushes, a large ground with a beautiful serpentine walk shaded with pines, firs, cedars, apple, pear, peach and plum trees, a long cedar hedge from the back to the front fence, with good health, clear head, grateful heart and ready hand, — what can I not do when surrounded by influences like these? What can I leave undone with so many aids?

Mr. Haines presented us with busts of Newton and Locke and our rooms are convenient and fitted up tastefully. A fine Venetian window looks down the yard at one end and two windows at the other end look into the main street. I have thus entered into details that you might have some notion of the premises.

Bronson did little letter writing that summer that concerned his daily life. He did tell his mother, though, under date of July 31, that "I am much interested in the progress of my little girl, now five months old, which I have recorded from the day of her birth. This record has swollen to a hundred pages. I have attempted to discourse, so far as this could be done by external indication, the successive steps of her physical, mental and moral advancement. The result has been to collect a much greater number of what seem to me facts than I at first imagined possible."

He read enormously during this period; Plato, Aristotle, Bacon, Carlyle, Coleridge, Bulwer's novels, Shelley's poetry and countless philosophical writers whose names mean little to us now. He took his school of twenty children for rides along the Wissahickon River and watched their reactions with the same keen eye that was recording Anna's growth. He was learning more and more about handling the young. Fall found him with as many children as he could handle. Then, in October, the unexpected blow fell. Friend Haines died, leaving the school without endowment.

Abba and Bronson, impractical souls, grieved at first only because they had lost a friend whom they loved. It was not until the school started to dwindle in numbers that they began to realize that the sturdy Quaker had subsidized them at both ends. He had inveigled his friends into sending their children to the school, then he had made up the deficit in salaries left by the low tuition fees.

But they carried on for a year, little by little cutting down expenses, the servants going first, until Abba was doing all of the housework and Bronson all of the chores. They had no sense of defeat although Abba lost some of her high spirits. She was not without justification for this, however, for on November 29, 1832, the second of the Little Women was born, Louisa May. On that day, Bronson wrote to his father-in-law:

Dear Sir: — It is with great pleasure that I announce to you the birth of a second daughter. She was born at half past twelve this morning on my birthday (33) and is a very fine healthful child, much more so than Anna was at birth, — has a fine foundation for health and energy of character. Abba is very comfortable and will soon be restored to the discharge of those domestic and maternal duties in which she takes so much delight and in the performance of which she furnishes so excellent a model for imitation. Those only who have seen her in those relations, much as there is in her general character to admire and esteem, can form a true estimate of her personal worth and uncommon devotion of heart. She was formed for domestic sentiment rather than the gaze and heartlessness of what is falsely called "society." Abba is inclined to call the baby Louisa May — a name to her full of every association connected with amiable benevolence and exalted worth.

I hope its present possessor may rise to equal attainment and deserve a place in the estimation of society.

With Abba's and Anna's and Louisa's regards, allow me to assure you of the sincerity with which I am,

                    Yours,

                    A. Bronson Alcott.

Though she crowded so closely on the advent of the small Anna, Louisa received a glorious welcome from her mother and father. Bronson took Anna into the schoolroom with him where she seemed not to detract one whit from the charm he held for his pupils and Abba, recovering perhaps less quickly from this second effort than she had from the first, found great joy in the dark-haired, robust child so like herself, whom she was obliged to leave much alone in her cradle while household duties crowded on the maternal.

But the school did dwindle, though for a long time Bronson refused to recognize this. Abba found it hard sometimes to curb her quick tongue when her husband appeared oblivious to the fact that there had been no meat in the house for two days and that the little boarding pupils were complaining. She let go, finally, when the third child within a week was removed by indignant parents.

"You must use common sense as well as theory when you are caring for children's bodies as well as their souls, Bronson. Don't you see that children need meat ? I need it myself ; don't you see that I can't bear children and work like a servant, on bread, water and hope deferred ?"

Bronson, who was pacing the floor with Louisa in his arms while thinking out his next lecture, stopped astounded before the fire, where his wife was making Anna ready for bed.

"What would you have me do, my dear ?" he gasped. "Can I hunt or trap in Germantown ? We have no money for the butcher."

"Close out this school before it plunges us hopelessly in debt and take up William Russell's idea of a school with him in Philadelphia. A boarding school is impossible, Bronson, if I am to do all the work."

Bronson returned to pacing the floor. Another failure! He might as well face it. Germantown was not ready for his ideas. But how wonderfully the children had responded ! He looked toward his desk where lay a little pile of manuscripts: letters and stories written by his pupils. He knew that never before had children of that age turned out work of such apparent precocity. His system worked! Yet he must leave these pupils mid-flight in their training and allow them to be submerged in the mediocrity for which their parents clamored.

Yet Abba was right. They were all of them hungry. He came back to her reluctantly. His lips quivered as he said quietly, "I 'll go talk to William Russell to-night."

Abba laid Anna in her cradle and turned to clasp her husband and the sleeping Louisa in her tender arms.

"Philadelphia knows you. You 'll not regret the decision, my dearest husband," she said.

Nor did he regret it, although Philadelphia, too, finally withdrew its children from him. He was growing to understand that immediate and permanent success was not for him and he was becoming inured to the thought. The school in Philadelphia established in March, 1833, lasted until the fall of 1834. In the latter part of 1833, Bronson wrote in his diary:

The nature of the experiment in which I am to engage, removed from popular appreciation, is in itself a bar to success. There are only a few who duly appreciate the ends or understand the means

96

by which the advancement of humanity is to be attained. The few are in the darkness of twilight regarding the whole matter and the mass of mankind wholly in the dark; often so fraught with prejudice and false opinion — with zeal without knowledge or knowledge without zeal — that a generous plan for the improvement of men would excite opposition and the worst form of sectarian jealousy. The fear of innovation — the idea of crumbling away the old foundation of opinion or practice — weighs down whatever promises well to mankind.

Boston seems adapted to my purposes better than any other city. Purer views of man prevail there, society is riper, intellectual and moral wealth are more equally diffused and the experiments made there on man and opinion have prepared the way for those I have in view. There, too, is a more intelligent sympathy for the improvement of humanity, freer toleration of variant opinions and a more generous philanthropy than can be found elsewhere.

It was true that Boston was taking a greater interest in the things Bronson had written about education than Philadelphia. Doctor Channing, the great Unitarian, Elizabeth Peabody, a Greek pupil of Emerson, Emerson himself, and many others whose fame has proved less permanent were urging the Alcotts to come back to Boston.

Bronson and Abba were only too eager to come. The circle of people in Philadelphia who took an interest in the new education was very small. And these two looked upon Boston as their Mecca, as the one spot where the soil lay waiting for the reception and rich cultivation of Bronson's ideas. What they did not realize, these two babes of the intellectual woods, was that Boston's interest in matters of mind and soul always has been that of the vivisectionist, and that it always has been capable of decisions as prejudiced as they are cruel, and cruel as they are violent.

But Bronson's probation period was ended. He had served nearly a ten-years' apprenticeship at teaching. He was the father of two children. He was the husband of a woman whom he was to love ardently until the day of his death. He had suffered and starved for his idea. It seemed as if life had completed her testing and embellishing and was willing to give the completed product to the world.

So on a beautiful summer day there disembarked in Boston from the Philadelphia steamer an extraordinarily interesting group of people. There was a tall man, blond, with a beautiful, gentle face; a tall woman with splendid dark eyes, and brilliant coloring, each of them carrying a child. The larger child of three in her father's arms was blonde like him, and she looked about her with the same placid, humorous eyes. The smaller child, of two, in her mother's arms, was a replica of her mother. She jumped and wriggled in the strong, tender arms, begged to be put down and stared with brilliant, stormy eyes at the crowds about her. Little Louisa May Alcott had come to the Boston that after many years was to take her to its heart and that was to repudiate and crucify her father.

CHAPTER VI

The Temple School

BRONSON was no longer in the experimental stage in the fall of 1834. He had a full and rounded programme of instruction carefully worked out in all details. And it was by no means an inexpensive programme. It required, beside Bronson, teachers of the highest intellectual order and a setting of beauty, even luxury.

Backed by the strong influence of Doctor Channing, Bronson was able to begin his school with what he felt were all the requisites of success. He procured as his assistant and teacher of Latin, Miss Elizabeth Peabody who was, thirty years later, to introduce the Kindergarten to America. She was about thirty years of age at this time. Her sisters — Sophia, who married Nathaniel Hawthorne, and Mary, who married Horace Mann — also assisted in the school, at need. Washington Allston, a distinguished artist of the day, directed the art work of the school, although Bronson himself attended to the details of this,

STEPHENS COLLEGE
LIBRARY

having a great deal of natural drawing ability. Margaret Fuller, coeditor with Emerson, of the *Dial*, taught intermittently at the school. Abba took charge of the music.

School was begun in the Masonic Temple on Tremont Street, then one of the finest buildings in Boston. We will let Bronson tell his own story:

Sept. 22, 1834. I opened to-day with thirty children (between three and twelve) and am assisted in their instruction by Miss Elizabeth Peabody whose reputation both as regards original and acquired ability is high, — she unites intellectual and practical qualities of no common order. Her proposition to aid me comes from the deep interest she feels in human culture, and her friendly desire to establish me in this city. I have obtained very fine rooms in the temple and have made arrangements to fit up the interior in a style corresponding to the exterior and what is of more importance, in adaptation to those who are to assemble there for the formation of tastes and habits.

I have spared no expense to surround the senses with appropriate emblems of intellectual and spiritual life. Painting, busts, books, and not inelegant furniture have been deemed important. I wish to fill every form that addresses the senses with significance and life, so that whatever is seen, said or done shall picture ideal beauty and perfection, thus placing the child in a scene of tranquil repose and spiritual loveliness. I would bring external circumstances into harmony with that serenity of spirit and vivacity of portraiture which are the native attributes of unspoiled childhood, — planting, as it were, a prop round which tendrils may fasten, and thus lift its aspiring energies to the skies.

My pupils seem favored by nature with good capacities. I am glad to find them so free from the usual entailment of school habits. They seem to have been well taught, having few vicious tendencies either of spirit or body. About half are girls, — a circumstance most favorable to the exertion of a pure and fine moral influence on the formation of character, and preserving the social relations unbroken during the impressionable period of life.

By the present arrangement, I shall never be occupied with practical instruction more than five hours daily, and ultimately, perhaps, not more than three. I shall be able also to do better justice to my family than I have done. Thirty pupils (there will doubtless be more) will bring me an income of $1800, — sufficient to support us comfortably and soon free me from debt. The sensation of thrift is to me a delightful one and the more so from the continuous suffering with untoward circumstances to which I have been subjected.

This income may at least take from the toil of life some anxieties and some impediments to progress in the celestial life and may serve to open out powers which have struggled amid severer conditions.

Oct. 11, 1834. I now have thirty-four pupils and most are under ten years of age. They make a happy, interesting group; they begin to take a deep interest in my teaching and to appreciate the purposes I have in view. They are a fine assemblage of children. There are few or no positive vices to eradicate; frivolity, carelessness, inactivity of thought and ill-directed desire are the main qualities to which my attention is to be turned. As to direct intellectual action, little can be expected immediately. I shall first remove obstructions to the growth of the mind; these lie in the appetites, passions, desires and will. Intellectual results will follow the discipline of the sentiments, for in these lie the guiding energies of the whole being.

He who reaches the will and subdues the desires, brings the child under his control and commences the work of human culture on a basis that will sustain and continue. The heart is the seat of action, — material, organic, intellectual, moral — influence this and the whole being feels the touch. To "keep this with all diligence" is the purpose of education, "for out of it are the issues of life."

103

"Obey and know" is the only maxim that leads to excellence. Faith imparts energy, growth, productiveness, to every germ of man's nature.

Oct. 23, 1834. In the discharge of my duties as a teacher, I have found very few works to aid me; I have been thrown mostly on my own resources, and have created, from circumstances and the ideal of my own mind, the material for intellectual and spiritual nurture. Very few works have become established favorites with children, — works containing thoughts to which they recur with delight and which waken, as it were, a brood of others in their mind and affect their habits both of feeling and of action. I mention as occurring to me at this time, the following: the Bible, Pilgrim's Progress, Krummacher's Parables, the Story Without End, Spenser's Fairy Queen, Quarle's Emblems, and Emblems, Moral and Divine (Alciat ?). To form a large library suitable to the wants of the young, from works among us would be impossible.

We have none, absolutely none, that nurture the spiritual life: for the moral nurture we have little. A dozen volumes would include all that is adequate to quicken and sustain the purest wants of the soul. On subjects of mere fancy or of the understanding we have many works; but they mostly serve to dissipate the thoughts of the young and materialize their spirits. I have been seeking works fit for my pupils for the past ten years and have found but few, — my library is still scanty; and yet in this period, hundreds of volumes have been added to our juvenile literature on almost every subject. In our indiscriminate zeal or blind indifference, we have either pampered or starved the young in this respect.

I have sent to England for copies of Pilgrim's Progress and the Fairy Queen: since fine copies of neither could be found in Boston at the common bookstores or the antiquarian shops of which there are two. Except in my own school, I know of no provision for the cultivation of the imagination by specific tuition anywhere in the country: I seldom hear anyone speak of the importance of cultivating it. And yet, if any fact be settled by history, it is that imagination is the guiding impulse of society.

For what is genius but this faculty in mind action? And genius has shaped the common mind and institutions in all ages. We need schools not for the inculcation of knowledge, merely, but for the development of genius; this is the peculiar attribute of the soul, — it is the soul, indeed, in full and harmonious play. And no instruction discerns the name that does not call forth this essential life of the soul and fit it for manifestation in literature, art or philosophy.

At my school, the spiritual fire begins to warm some of the drowsy, cold natures into life and

movement, but I have yet much to
succeeded in interesting all, have
understanding of all and am feeling
their hearts. I am vivifying the in
the affections will come along with
of the older ones require great changes
before the understanding, the heart
can act with freedom and accuracy.

Here are young beginnings who ha
or twelve years and have not yet lear
conditions of spiritual progress, — wh
obedience and application are all
improvement. They are sunk in th
the currents of the will are set again
and the spirit. Much less needs to
the younger pupils than for these.

Discipline! Discipline! Discipline
intellectual! The younger pupils are
a rigidity, a frowardness, has not yet
duced; such are still the yielding su
cipline. There must have been great
where. A depraved child! Never w
when parental and social influence
bestowed upon it. But of human cul
as yet very little; little of the being w
office to cultivate; and the sad story
rance is told and constantly repeated
perversity of man's noble powers.
stop to listen, — we have become so a

106

works fit for my pupils for the past ten years and have found but few, — my library is still scanty; and yet in this period, hundreds of volumes have been added to our juvenile literature on almost every subject. In our indiscriminate zeal or blind indifference, we have either pampered or starved the young in this respect.

I have sent to England for copies of Pilgrim's Progress and the Fairy Queen: since fine copies of neither could be found in Boston at the common bookstores or the antiquarian shops of which there are two. Except in my own school, I know of no provision for the cultivation of the imagination by specific tuition anywhere in the country: I seldom hear anyone speak of the importance of cultivating it. And yet, if any fact be settled by history, it is that imagination is the guiding impulse of society.

For what is genius but this faculty in mind action? And genius has shaped the common mind and institutions in all ages. We need schools not for the inculcation of knowledge, merely, but for the development of genius; this is the peculiar attribute of the soul, — it is the soul, indeed, in full and harmonious play. And no instruction discerns the name that does not call forth this essential life of the soul and fit it for manifestation in literature, art or philosophy.

At my school, the spiritual fire begins to warm some of the drowsy, cold natures into life and movement, but I have yet much to do. I have succeeded in interesting all, have reached the understanding of all and am feeling my way to their hearts. I am vivifying the imaginations: the affections will come along with this. Some of the older ones require great changes to be made before the understanding, the heart or the mind can act with freedom and accuracy.

Here are young beginnings who have lived ten or twelve years and have not yet learned the first conditions of spiritual progress, — whose views of obedience and application are all adverse to improvement. They are sunk in the senses and the currents of the will are set against the heart and the spirit. Much less needs to be done for the younger pupils than for these.

Discipline! Discipline! Discipline, moral and intellectual! The younger pupils are still docile; a rigidity, a frowardness, has not yet been superinduced; such are still the yielding subjects of discipline. There must have been great neglect somewhere. A depraved child! Never was there one when parental and social influences were duly bestowed upon it. But of human culture we know as yet very little; little of the being whom it is our office to cultivate; and the sad story of our ignorance is told and constantly repeated in the early perversity of man's noble powers. We do not stop to listen, — we have become so accustomed to the tale that we deem this a necessary appendage to our life.

Jan. 3, 1834. In addition to the statuary and painting at the schoolroom, I added to-day a fine cast of Silence from some Italian model. It was executed by some Italian in School Street and is, I conceive, quite an acquisition to the school. It will aid me in the work of discipline. I will here enumerate the casts, busts and pictures placed in my schoolroom: Head of Jesus in basso relievo: bust of Plato: bust of Socrates on pedestal: bust of Milton, on pedestal: picture of Dr. Channing, by Harding: picture of travelers: picture of a rural scene: picture of the Flight into Egypt, by Guido (an engraving): picture of the Temple (an engraving): casts of the Sciences, by Canova: cast of Silence.

Besides these works of art, often called into use as illustrations of subjects of instruction, and tending to impress the sense of reality upon the mind of the pupil, the schoolroom is fitted with tasteful furniture, desk, chairs, books, tablets (paper and wooden), cubes, cards, clock, with an alarm for the hours of study, hour-glass, dissected letters, mirror, boxes, vases, etc., the whole diffusing unconsciously an influence favorable to tranquillity, thought and study. The effect of the external arrangements is so much aid in the work of discipline, intellectual and moral. Happiness, application, are the most natural results of these influences. The mind is predisposed to repose and serenity; and the instruction, harmonizing with the external influences, renders the school a delightful place in their associations.

Miss Peabody is now present, every day, and keeps a journal of the operations and spirit of the instruction. It bids fair to prove a faithful transcript of what passes in the classroom. This journal is to be published, not only as a prospectus of my present school but as an offering to the community of the fruits of my mind on a most important relation : for I do not wish to come forward with an elaborate work on the philosophy and practice of education. The time has not yet come. Principles and methods, what is theoretic and what is practical, should be united at present in whatever is thrown out to the inquisitive public. A simple record of practice in the schoolroom, with just enough explanation to make it intelligible, to impart the spirit of the theory will be more effective in impressing my views than a more elaborate work.

The public was inquisitive and long before the "Record of a School" was published, it had investigated Bronson and his work. The first reaction was extraordinarily enthusiastic. The intellectuals of Boston haunted the Temple School and found it wonderful. A protégé of Doctor Channing was bound to get a fair hearing. But more than that, Bronson had married into a Unitarian family of influence, had himself become a Unitarian and this alone in those days was sufficient to establish him as a man of brain. More than that, he was beautiful to look upon and a brilliant conversationalist, while his wife was handsome, witty, vivacious and a perfect hostess.

It became the correct thing for visiting foreigners to be taken to visit the Temple School. Richard Henry Dana, author of "Two Years Before the Mast", took Miss Harriet Martineau, the noted English reformer and litterateur, there. Ralph Waldo Emerson, who had not yet achieved fame but was a man of a certain influence, haunted the school and took elaborate notes for his own diary of Bronson's conversations. He also invited Bronson to Concord and wrote of the event:

Oct. 21, 1835. Last night came hither Mr. Alcott and spent the Sabbath, — a wise man, simple, superior to display and drops the best things as quietly as the least. Every man, he says, is a revelation and ought to write his own record, but few with the pen. *His* book is his School, in which he writes all his thoughts. The spiritual world should meet men anywhere and so the government should teach. Our life flows out into amusements. Need of a drama here: how well to lash the American follies. Every man is a system, an institution; autobiography the best book. He thinks Jesus is a pure deist and says all children are deists.

June 16, 1836. Yesterday, I went to Mr. Alcott's school and heard a conversation upon the Gospel of John. I thought the experiment of engaging young children upon questions of taste and truth successful. A few striking things were said by them. I felt strongly as I watched the gradual dawn of a thought upon the minds of all, that to Truth is no age or season. It appears or it does not appear: and when the child perceives it, he is no more a child. Age, sex are nothing: we are all alike before the great Whole. Little Josiah Quincy, now six years six months old, is a child having something wonderful and divine in him. He is a youthful prophet.

Emerson wrote to W. H. Furness in October, 1836:

I shall always love you for loving Alcott. He is a great man; the good with the herdsmen of Admetus. I cannot think you know him now, when I remember how long he has been here for he gains every month. His conversation is sublime.

CHAPTER VII

Anna and Louisa

BRONSON's diary at this time, however, was by no means entirely given to school matters. He was setting down in it the gradually developing ideas on religion that were making him the leader of Transcendentalism in Boston. And continuing the work begun in Philadelphia he was setting down the touching record of his children's lives.

Observations on the Spiritual Nature of my Children (Anna and Louisa) 1834–5. On these pages I will trace the glimpses that may be vouchsafed me from the Inner Life of their Spirits. Dimly shall I see — vaguely shall I apprehend, the lights and shadows of their Inner Life — for I have strayed away from the orb that illumines and am a wanderer in the darkness of the outer Existence ; — not lost, but in the twilight ; the ray that will, perhaps, lead me to the Place where the Ideal is, for the "Star hath appeared and stood over it."

Monday, October 27, 1834. . . . I dressed them this morning at an early hour. Louisa shed a few tears while being dressed. She has been less irritable, I understand from her mother, than usual. She enjoyed Anna's society with several of the little ones at school for an hour. She took a nap at noon : went to bed, shedding tears. Her mother deemed it best to discipline her into silence, crying on going to bed being one of her almost confirmed habits.

Anna spent some time with me after tea, in the study. She was remarkably amiable, communicative. But she did not succeed in getting to bed without tears, her common habit, if urged against her will. I punished her, sending her to bed without a kiss and shutting the door of her bed chamber. . . .

Louisa's deep-seated obstinacy of temper is far from being conquered. She is by no means docile. Submission is an act of self-inflection that she renders doubly painful by her resistance to every entreaty. I find that the readier way is to let her rage against herself in cases of personal evil ; the simplest request made in gentlest tone, leads to reaction when her spirit is ardent in pursuit of some favorite object, as when ruffled by disappointment or opposition from her sister. I have not resorted to physical suffering today, remindings of the possibility of punishment having succeeded in controlling her. . . .

She has not been without her tranquil hours,

however. In moods of quiet, when all around her is in harmony with her self-relying spirit, she is most interesting. I had a long interview with her after she had laid herself in bed. Her thoughts come rushing after each other with a vivid celerity, so fast and so evanescent both in idea and expression that 't was almost impossible to fasten them in the mind. The attention refused to stay them in their passing by. They were all clear and vivid to her: each had a local habitation and a name, a shape in her imagination, a sentiment in her spirit. Her reactions are dramatic, Anna's, owing to the reflective quality of her mind, are epic.

. . . Louisa is making rapid progress in spoken Language. She adds new words to her vocabulary daily. I believe she appreciates *all* the relations of expression, using every part of speech. . . . She is very pantomimic; gesture, countenance, forming no inept types of her ideas and sentiments. Anna depends more on words. Her vocabulary is large for a child of her years. . . .

Vulgarity and impurity of association is doubtless the product of a *dimmed* and *degraded* ideal. The spirit of a child has no associations formed on senses or the objects and relations of the outer world: there are none but celestial forms in his spirit at first. And if, as his mind opens and seeks to express itself, impure ideas, gross sentiments are found struggling for utterance, it will be owing not to innate impurity or inborn depravity but to the emblems and words by which he has been addressed. . . . Children take what is offered them. If they are fed on impure or degrading nurture, the spirit will suffer therefrom. Life external is the nurse and feeder of the internal life. A pure taste is the product of a pure imagination, quickened and vivified by life. The arts — society — are the representations of this taste of the spirit. Nurse the spirit in purity and cherish its innocence and all its issues will bespeak its virginity. Parents have a responsibility in this respect undreampt of as yet. . . .

They are much delighted with dramatic pastimes, particularly after tea. They spend an hour, at twilight, usually, in this active way. Among the pastimes most attractive — stock pieces on their little theatre — are Wilson's Snow Storm, in which Louisa is very successful in personating the character of Hannah Lee, left in the snow — the old woman and the peddler (a profound drama on personal identity), Little Henri and the Gypsies. These are personated every evening and with ever new delight. The accompaniment of music and dancing are also super-added. The hour before going to bed is uniformly devoted to these embodyings of the Ideal: after which comes the Story and they pass from the world of sleep, to enjoy the full ideal. . . .

I had a long conversation with them today. We were speaking of love when Anna said,

"Father, I don't love you as well as I do mother."

"Aye!" said I, "I should like to be loved as much as Mother. I suppose, when I am as good as Mother, you will love me as much. Don't you think you shall?"

"Yes, Father, I think I shall."

"But Anna, why am I not as good as Mother? What have I done? I wish you would tell me, so that I may try to make you love me as much as you do her. Do you think you can tell me?"

"You punish me, Father, and Mother does not."

"Aye, that is the reason then! Well, should not naughty girls, naughty children — be punished to make them better?"

"Yes, Father."

"Well, cannot you love Father, who punishes you to make you dislike your naughtinesses?"

"Well, Father, I like you both, sometimes, and sometimes I do not like you both. But you are both good!"

. . . Anna mentioned to me the fact of Louisa's hurting her. — I called Louisa to me and said, "Louisa, Anna says you took hold of her hair so" (pulling it, while she looked into my face with a prying curiosity to discover whether I was punishing her or only showing her, being somewhat dubious of me from the tone of my voice and the expression of my countenance), "and," I continued, "that you pinched her cheek, so —" (pinching it).

She hesitated a moment whether to mind the pain or not. At last the fortitude prevailed and she said, "Father, I was naughty to hurt Anna so."

"Yes, Louisa, and what has father been doing to you?"

"Hurting me," said she.

"Why?"

"Because I was naughty," said she.

"And did you hurt Anna because she was naughty?"

"No," said she, perceiving the object of my question.

"Father hurt Louisa to show her how she hurt Anna. Did you know that you hurt her so when you pulled and pinched?"

She made no answer, but she understood me.

. . .

Both required punishment this morning to bring their wills into a docile state. They rose in a state of disquiet. Anna was querulous, Louisa turbulent. I spanked them both, Anna with some severity. She was brought to herself by this discipline and behaved well all day. The effect was good on Louisa, too. . . . The children passed the morning in the nursery with their mother, engaged, as usual, in enacting their ideals. Fully employed were they, busy at the ever moving wheel of life, whose revolving spokes carry them, not without a dubious consciousness, around the cycle of time and over the dominion of space. And who turneth the wheel? Doth not the Divinity himself? Doth not He stand by and witness the essaying wills that struggle always against or with the inspiration that carryeth, whether the soul will or not, the wheel of life onward toward its destination? . . .

CHAPTER VIII

The "Record of a School"

DAY by day for over a year Miss Peabody set down the school happenings. She explained in her introduction that it was not possible to report verbatim both Mr. Alcott's words and those of the children. She was not a stenographer. So she chose to give the children's exact words and paraphrased Mr. Alcott's whenever necessary. This explanation was made, Miss Peabody said, in reply to critics who declared that as reported in the *Record*, children could not understand the teacher's language.

One reads the story of the school with wonder at the long, long distance traveled by that little boy from Spindle Hill.

The oldest pupil was a boy just under twelve years of age, the youngest, little Anna Bronson Alcott, three, with Louisa an occasional visitor. The children, on the opening morning, said Miss Peabody, were inclined to be unruly. One or two of the older boys were impertinent. But this

STEPHENS COLLEGE
LIBRARY

THE TEMPLE SCHOOL

was not the young teacher of Cheshire days who romped and played with his pupils. Bronson had developed an invaluable quality in teaching. Gentle and tranquil as he was, there was a steel core to his softness and the children had not been with him an hour before they felt it.

Said Miss Peabody:

It was soon found that Mr. Alcott, with all his mildness was very strict. When sitting at their writing, he would not allow the least inter-communication and every whisper was taken notice of. The desks were placed against the wall, around the room, so that the children, when studying, had their backs to Mr. Alcott and also did not see one another. When reciting, the children sat in an arc about his desk in very comfortable chairs, placed so far apart that the children could not easily touch one another.

When they sat in this semi-circle, they were not only requested to be silent but to appear attentive to him; and any infringement of this rule would interrupt his reading and he would wait, however long it might be, until order was restored. For instance, the acquirement of this habit of stillness and attention was the most prominent object; for it was found that many of the children had very little self-control, very weak attention, very self-indulgent habits.

Some had no humility and defended themselves in the wrong : there was some correction, but still, in every instance, it was granted as necessary not only by the whole school, but it never was given without the assent of the individual himself and never given in the room. Sometimes, in the pauses of the reading, for instance, the innocent were obliged to suffer with the guilty. Mr. Alcott wished both parties to feel that this was the inevitable consequence of moral evil in the world and that the good, in proportion to the depth of their principle, feel it worth while to share the suffering in order to bring the guilty to rectitude and moral sensibility. . . .

A great deal of time was spent, from the first, in explaining the philosophy of Expression. They were taught to see that sculpture, painting and words were only different modes of expression. . . . They led to consider how words body forth thoughts, signing external objects and suggesting internal facts of the spirit. External fact was discriminated from internal truth and the youngest children were exercised on such questions as these : Is *love* in the mind or out of the mind ? Is a *book* in the mind or out of the mind ? Is a *table* in the mind or out of the mind ? They were soon able to answer and seldom made a mistake, especially the younger ones.

One great means, however, of making this subject thoroughly understood, was by reading to them and fastening their attention, and then bringing them to attend the fact of having been thus chained to their chairs by thoughts and feelings in their own minds which words had waked up. As Mr. Alcott read, his eyes sought all their faces : a wandering mind was immediately detected and he required them at any moment he might choose to stop to repeat to him in their own language what he had last said, to describe the picture he was calling up or to give the meaning of the allegory. And as the matter was intensely interesting, taken from the master works of genius, he succeeded in gaining attention, also its outward signs. They were soon able to catch the meaning of emblems so as to preclude the necessity for explanation.

Here one observes how closely Bronson's educational ideas and his religious growth were beginning to overlap. In a letter to Miss Peabody, he said :

Emblems I have found to be extremely attractive to children. I could not teach without them. My own mind would suffer were it not nurtured upon ideas in this form and spiritual instruction is best imparted by these means. The universal spirit flows into man and nature through these media and sense and imagination are the faculties that receive the divine stream — the one from without and the other from within — and from it upon the soul. The manner of Jesus and of Plato is authority, if any were needed, to show what a mind requires in order to be quickened and renewed! Without a parable spake he not unto them? Neither should the teacher of spiritual truth nowadays.

Miss Peabody goes on:

It was in the pursuance of these ideas that Mr. Alcott took so much pains at first to bring out clearly in children's consciousness a conception of the spiritual world, as alone having permanence and reality, not withstanding its invisibleness. And when he read he constantly asked questions calculated to keep attention on the ideas in the author's mind that were clothed with imagery or signed by words. So successful was he in fixing attention on the spiritual part of any matter, that not only the imagery of poetry but every incident of a narrative, was listened to with an air of thought and investigation not always seen in adult hearers of reading. . . .

Mr. Alcott thinks every book read should be an event to a child; and all his plans of reading keep steadily in view the object of making books live, breathe and speak and he considers the glib reading in some schools a prevention rather than an aid to his purposes.

The first two months of the school were given up almost entirely to this preliminary discipline. Two hours and a half every day were divided between the readings and conversations on conduct and the comparative importance of things within and without. The government was decided and clear from the first but was not hurried beyond the comprehension of the children. Mr. Alcott's autocracy is drawn from experience and observations and I should add, continually takes counsel from its success. And is not this a legitimate autocracy in the moral sense of the word?

When he first began to teach school, he thought no punishment was desirable and spent much time in reasoning. But besides that this consumed a great deal of time that might better have been spent, he became convinced that the passions cannot in all cases be met by an address to the understanding and were only diverted and not conquered by being reasoned with. What would excite feeling, he found, must be brought to bear upon wrong feeling when that actually existed, and to arouse sensibility when there was a deficiency.

Deeper observations of life and of human nature convinced him that the ministry of pain was God's great means of developing strength and elevation of character and that children should early understand this, that they might accept it as a moral blessing. He therefore introduced punishment by name and found that in theorizing on the subject with his scholars, there was a general feeling of its desirableness and necessity and he never failed in obtaining their consent to it as a general principle. Corporal punishment was administered in the ante-room: though he made an exception once when one of the oldest boys wantonly disobeyed, for the purpose of displaying to his companions his daring spirit and needed the mortification of seeing himself humbled before the rest.

After two months of probation and preliminary training, Bronson introduced a daily programme.

Miss Peabody's record of each day's events does not contain a dull page:

January 16, 1835. At ten minutes past ten the spelling lesson began after he had placed the chairs of the smaller division very far apart from each other, so that the children would not be tempted to whisper. . . . When the word *vast* was defined, Mr. Alcott asked if the idea of vastness was within or without. Some said within. One hesitated and Mr. Alcott asked what was vast? He said the ocean. Mr. Alcott asked if the ocean did not wake up the idea of vastness in his mind. He replied, yes, and so vastness is in the mind. What, then, is the ocean? asked Mr. Alcott. An emblem of vastness, said the boy. The ocean then is the

The Tuition and Discipline are addressed in due proportion to the threefold Nature of Childhood

THE SPIRITUAL FACULTY (Means of direct Culture)
- Listening to Sacred Readings
- Conversations on the Gospels
- Writing Journals
- Self-analysis and Self Discipline
- Listening to readings from works of genius
- Motives to study and action
- Government of the School

THE IMAGINATIVE FACULTY (Means of Direct Culture)
- Spelling and Reading
- Writing and sketching from nature
- Picturesque geography
- Writing Journals and epistles
- Illustrating words
- Listening to readings
- Conversation

THE RATIONAL FACULTY (Means of direct Culture)
- Defining Words
- Analyzing words
- Self-analysis
- Arithmetic
- Study of the Human Body
- Reasoning on conduct
- Discipline

TIME	MONDAY	TUESDAY	WEDNESDAY	THURSDAY	FRIDAY	SATURDAY
IX	Studying Spelling and Defining and Writing in Journals	Studying Geography and Sketching maps in Journals	Studying the Gospel and writing in Journals	Studying parsing lesson and writing in Journal	Paraphrasing text of reading and writing in Journals	Completing of account of weeks study in Journals
X XI	Spelling with illustrative conversations on the meaning and uses of words	Recitations in Geography with Picturesque readings and conversations	Readings and conversations on Spirit as displayed in the life of Christ	Analyzing speech written and vocal on tablets with illustrative conversations	Readings with illustrative conversations on the sense of the text	Readings from works of genius with applications and conversations
		RECREATION	ON THE COMMON	OR IN THE	ANTE-ROOM	
XII I	Studying arithmetic with demonstrations in Journals	Drawings from nature with Mr. Graeter	Conversations on the human body and its culture	Composing and writing epistles in journals	Studying arithmetic with illustrations in journals	Review of journal, Week's Conduct and Studies
		INTERMISSION	FOR REFRESHMENT	AND RECREATION		
III IV	Studying Latin and Writing in Journals	Studying Latin with Recitations	Recreation and duties at home	Studying Latin with recitations	Studying Latin and Writing in Journals	Recitations and Duties at Home

external, visible, material sign, type of emblem of the internal, invisible, spiritual idea of vastness: is it? The definition was repeated in nearly the same words by two of the class.

The word *veil* led to the consideration of the body as the veil of the spirit and the earth as the veil of the ideas of God. When was the veil of sense wrapped around our souls? asked Mr. Alcott. When we were born, said one. When will it be taken away? When we die, said several. Cannot the veil be raised until we die? After a while, it was seen and said that the veil could be raised by being born again out of sense into thought or spirit, — by insight. Mr. Alcott then said that the object of this school was to unveil the soul; and he was glad to hear that one of the scholars had said, out of school, that it was impossible to remain in it and not to learn to know one's self.

He then took up the word *work*, in every variety of application, literal and figurative and he went on in this talk, bringing in every word of the spelling lesson in various meanings. *Yelk*, he said, was the food by which the germ of life was nourished into the power of forming a body that might individualize it: and he said the earth (perhaps) was the yelk by which souls were nourished or born into a consciousness of the spiritual life. He explained this a little. All eyes were fixed upon him, almost constantly. Neither a sense of duty alone, nor the attraction of the speaker alone, could explain the profound attention of these children. But the combination of the two causes is irresistible. And Mr. Alcott required them to seem attentive as well as to be attentive. He often talks to them on the possibility and the duty of making every part of their body express the thought of their minds and tells them they must not accuse people of injustice who interpret their automatic movements as careless habits.

After Mr. Alcott had illustrated all the words of the lesson by this conversation, he took the dictionary and read Johnson's definitions, to see how much resemblance there was, and this led to further remarks on the words. He then heard the words spelled and asked each one to give a short definition.

While I was attending to the Latin, after recess, Mr. Alcott gave lessons in Arithmetic and English Grammar.

Jan. 17th. I arrived before nine and found some of the scholars at their desks and also heard some geometry lessons. Mr. Alcott then prepared to read in the Bible. I am going to read about One, said he, of whose thoughts, actions and feelings you always delight to hear; whom you are reminded of by that cast (pointing to Christ's head); for that is a representation of the body out of which he looked. All spirits in the world are in bodies: his was, just as your spirits are in your bodies. Well, this one said "I and my Father are one." He didn't mean one body but one spirit: that they had the same thoughts and feelings. All pure spirits, all real spirits, must have the same thoughts and feelings, must be one with God. Jesus soon had an opportunity to prove what he said about the spirit's being one with God. A friend of his died. It was the brother of Mary and Martha . . . Mr. Alcott paraphrased the whole story thus but I could not keep up with my pen. The children were profoundly attentive and deeply impressed. After this Mr. Alcott took the younger division of the spelling class. One of the boys said, "Mr. Alcott, I have learned my lesson," on which Mr. Alcott, taking up a book imitated the manner in which a child tried to study with the lips, without the mind.

They all laughed, and he then explained study to be thinking about words until pictures were formed in their minds and he ridiculed the humming, buzzing, whispering over the words, moving the body, etc., by imitating it himself. And when he asked if they understood him, if they agreed with his views, they agreed. He then described how this lesson should be studied, how they could think, beforehand, of illustrating the words in sentences and convinced them that to learn the spelling lesson thoroughly would require the whole hour assigned to it.

A girl then said, "Mr. Alcott, I wonder how it is that we sit here over the spelling lesson as long as we do in church and yet I never am the least fatigued, while in church I am so tired and we have to sit as still here as there." The rest agreed in wondering with her why it was. Mr. Alcott said it was because their minds were more active here, and activity of mind made the blood circulate and the whole body feel vigorous. He said it was one of his great objects to call forth the souls to govern the body. He spoke of manners and said that, for good manners, there must be both refined minds and the early acquired habit of letting the mind govern the body.

There was a talk with one boy who made an objection to the encroachment on the recess; and Mr. Alcott said that this boy thought it was wrong to lose one moment's play but he did not think it wrong to occupy ever so much time in school hours with unnecessary opposition. He said, were it not for his health, he should deprive him entirely of his recess on account of his encroachments upon the school hours.

January 22. I arrived late . . . then the younger division of the spelling lesson spelled and he told them to take their books and keep their fingers on the words as the rest of the class spelled and talked about them. The class turned and arranged themselves very quietly.

What ideas does the word *blade* bring into your minds? asked Mr. Alcott. A spear of grass and the part of the knife that cuts, said one. The next added, a gay young man; the next, a sword; the next, a scythe. Another boy said, a blade may be a figurative expression for the mind when it is sharpened by wisdom. Another said, the shoulder-blade. The next said, a pair of scissors. Mr. Alcott then read Johnson's definition and spoke of the blades of corn and quoted, "first the blade, then the ear, then the full corn in the ear."

What idea do you connect with the word *blame*? To reproach, said one. Blame is speaking ill of, said the next: and the next said to accuse one of being the means of something wrong being done. Mr. Alcott then read Johnson's definition and the definition of all the derivatives. Mr. Alcott said that it was a great character which could receive blame without resentment. One boy said he never could be blamed without being angry. . . Mr. Alcott asked two of the boys if they did not think that a few months before they were too apt to be angry when they were blamed and to defend themselves when they were really in the wrong? They both confessed. Mr. Alcott said they had entered the Wicket Gate and the burden had loosened from their backs: for that he never had seen children who were such extraordinary instances of the determination not to be found fault with: and that if they had got over that, they had accomplished more than as if they had learned a whole sentence.

Bliss was defined as the highest degree of pleasure. One boy remarked that pleasure once before had been defined as enjoyment of the body and happiness of the mind. Mr. Alcott said pleasure is the divinity of earth and bliss descends from heaven. After recess the children wrote in their diaries or journals.

Feb. 4. After the usual class work, Mr. Alcott read the poem, "Ode on the Intimations of Immortality", stopping as usual to explain and to get the children's ideas. At the line "Heaven lies about us in our infancy", he shut up the book and asked every child separately what he understood by a birth. They all answered and many repeated the definition which they gave the other day. Mr. Alcott observed that there was one striking difference in their answers: some expressed the idea that soul shaped and made the body, others that the body was made and the soul put into it. Which is right? asked a boy. That is more than I can tell, said Mr. Alcott, but I incline to the first opinion. I believe that birth is not the beginning of spirit. Life is the remembrance of what is already within, — "The rising of life's star, that elsewhere had its setting."

What is life's star? he asked. The soul, said they. But birth is sometimes the prelude to death of the soul, said Mr. Alcott. How? said one boy. Because, he replied, the soul becomes the slave of the body: is governed, darkened, shut up and buried in it and it is necessary that it should be born again. Some of you here have needed to be born again into your new life. . . .

Suppose we take the seed of a plant and put it in the ground. It bursts and some parts shoot down into the ground, and some up toward the light. Now, can you understand this, that the soul is a seed placed in the world, represented by the ground, and that the shoots that go down into the earth to fasten the plant in the ground, a while, are the bodily feelings and appetites: and that the shoots which grow upward toward the light are the affections and better feelings that seek Heaven? Do you understand? They said yes, quite breathlessly.

Well, suppose that more of the seed shoots down than is necessary and that no shoots go upward: would there be any flower and fruit? No, it would be all root: all would be under the earth. Well, can you understand that if the soul loves the body only and only uses its animal appetite and does not seek the light and Heaven, it will have no beauty or fruit, but will be an earthly, dark thing, a root ? Yes, they understood that.

Well, said he, now you know why I wish to check your animal appetites, your love of the body when that interferes with the mind's growth. It is right to love your body in a degree : the body has its uses : but it is one thing to take care of your body and another to indulge it. The plant must have root enough to make it stand steady in the earth. But that is enough.

Feb. 12. After arithmetic, the reading class read poetry. One boy, eight years old, read as his favorite lines :

"Thou are going home
Thy Father's face to see . . ."

Why is it said "Father's face" ? asked another boy. You can't see God's face. Mr. Alcott replied, Do you know that you never would have seen the outward world except by first going within yourself ? After a long pause of thought, the boy said, Yes, I see that. Then, asked Mr. Alcott, what do you see in any person's face beside the features ? The mind, the expressions of the soul, said the boy after some hesitation. And if God expresses himself in any way to us, said Mr. Alcott, when we go inward and think over our own faculties and feelings which are his expressions of love to us, is it not very natural to say we

133

have seen his face? I can't help thinking God has a real face, said another boy of eight. Can you think of your own spirit without thinking of a face, asked Mr. Alcott. Yes. Then why not think of God's spirit, said Mr. Alcott? I can, replied the boy. Do you think you see more of your brother when you see his body with your eyes or think about him in your mind? I think, replied the child, that I realize him when I think of him sometimes more than when I am looking at him.

CHAPTER IX

Theory and Practice

NOT only Miss Peabody and the other teachers but the many visitors to the school commented again and yet again on the enthralled interest the children took in this unique method of the study of spelling. Bronson's reply was always that he was greatly helped by the fact that no subject interests the growing child so much as self-analysis. To give name to the inner workings of his mind and heart interests the most volatile child. There is no one thing in external nature that interests all children. But every child is conscious of something within that thinks and feels and as a mere subject of investigation it takes precedence over all others for holding a child's attention.

Some of his critics said that the philosophy of the spirit was a disputed philosophy and therefore was not a subject for dogmatic teaching. Bronson replied to this that his teaching was not dogmatic, that nothing more was assumed by him than that spirit exists, bearing a relation to the body in which it is manifested, analagous to the relation which God bears to the external creation. And it was only those persons who were spiritual so far as to admit this whom he expected to place children under his care.

He was accused, at times, of teaching the Oriental doctrine of reincarnation. Miss Peabody made an emphatic denial of this.

Bronson, she said, indeed believed that birth is a spiritual act and fact prior to embodiment. But even this he did not teach dogmatically. It came out spontaneously from the children themselves and almost invariably as soon as they came to see the divine nature of the conscience and the sentiments. It is entirely against the spirit of Mr. Alcott's plan to dogmatize even on what he believes.

Indeed, it is almost impossible for any one who has not been in the school to understand how truly the opinion of others, even of Mr. Alcott, becomes a secondary object of attention with the children, after the mind has been opened into the region of ideas by the key of well understood words. There is real intellectual activity in these little minds and a pursuit of truth on true principles. This is often the case before it is evidenced by ready answers. It often happens that a child is some weeks and even months or a year at the school without say-

136

ing many things: but perfectly absorbed and attentive and giving a silent vote on all questions so decided. At last, he begins to speak and almost astonishes us by his thoughts and expressions. The journals which the children begin to keep as soon as they can join letters also often give indications of attention and interest before there is much said.

These journals are remarkable evidence of many angles of the effectiveness of Bronson's method of teaching: not least of the use of words. Following, for example, is an extract from the journal of a boy of ten, unedited.

Jan. 15, 1836. When I arrived at school this morning, I found a good many of the scholars there, and we began by singing Old Hundred, Mrs. Alcott playing on the piano and leading us with her voice, which I think is a very fine one. We sang for about a quarter of an hour, and then Mr. Alcott explained to us the meaning of the words we had just been singing, which I think were very interesting and characteristic. The reading was very interesting. It was about the visitation of God to Moses, from a thundercloud, on the top of Mount Sinai, and when he delivered to him the Commandments, which now appear to me much closer and more strict than before.

Feb. 24. Mr. Alcott read to us from the third chapter of John and the part I was most interested in was about a man's being born again. I was not very attentive the first part of the conversation, as I got thinking about other things, such as percussion caps, etc.; but the conversation soon interested me a great deal more than the percussion caps and other little things (which I was thinking about at first), and I soon became so interested in the conversation that I thought of nothing else. . . .

When Miss Peabody first went to the Temple School she did not approve of Bronson's idea of discipline. She had always taught girls, older than Bronson's pupils. Her theory and practice had been to handle each child individually, taking it for granted that in each there was the germ of a "sense of duty." Any dereliction she met with surprise, as an accidental mistake, and endeavored to win the pupil's confidence, that she might as a friend offer advice. She thus established a separate understanding with each scholar — a private understanding, for in general assembly no reference was made of wrong doing by any one. Courteously and charitably she took for granted that all meant to act conscientiously.

When she went to the Temple School, she said, she was full of these views, and inclined to believe them the only correct ones, though she admitted they were feasible only in a small school and that the amount of time required to establish the intimate relationship was huge and wearing. But Bronson forced her to consider another method.

Here was a school of thirty to sixty children, mostly boys under ten years of age, who, she said, "were creatures of instinct more than anything else, with undeveloped consciences and minds: well disposed, good natured, but overflowing with animal spirits and all but intoxicated with the idea of play." It was plain that Miss Peabody's plan could get no foothold here.

Bronson's first aim was the reverse of the individual. He wished to establish what he called the Treasury of the School. This was a common conscience. The common or general conscience, he claimed, would be higher than the individual. The soul when nearest infancy was the purest: the artlessness of children made them express their strongest convictions even when it made against themselves, and though the very young were apt to do wrong things, they did not defend wrong in the abstract.

From all this, he inferred that the moral judgments of the majority would be higher than their conduct, while the minority whose conduct was more in proportion to their moral judgment would still keep this high place and occasionally throw their finer elements into the general conscience, the treasury.

His applications of disciplinary means all were based on this. He chose or allowed the children to choose, each day, one of the pupils as a superintendent, the pupils agreeing to submit to any punishments Mr. Alcott might found on the superintendent's judgment. Miss Peabody trembled at first at the thought of such an experiment. But the result proved that the worst boys when put into such an office, became scrupulously just and got an idea of superintending themselves which nothing else could give.

The second step of the method was the habit of a general discussion of the conduct of individual scholars. To Miss Peabody's surprise, this developed in the children a degree of honesty, simplicity, self-surrender and general acknowledgment of a standard of action beyond the control of any individual such as no other school in the land, Miss Peabody declared, could show. "All false

140

pretensions, vanity, and self-exaltation are completely taken down." The majority of the school made moral progress which, considering their age, was beyond all parallel in her observation.

Among other criticisms on Bronson's intellectual methods was that " he neglected science for the far more difficult subject of spiritual analysis."

Bronson's reply was that however difficult soul analysis might be, science was still more difficult to grasp. The laws of the Eternal Spirit working in external nature were much more remote from the children's consciousness than were the emotional and moral laws to which he so often directed their attention.

He declared there was not a little illusion on the matter of teaching science to young children. If children learned the names of the stars, if they gathered flowers into herbariums, stones, minerals, shells, and insects into cabinets and witnessed some chemical experiments, they were supposed to have studied the sciences. "But astronomy does not consist of a list of the heavenly bodies but of the laws of their motions and interrelations : nor chemistry of the names of substances but of their combinations and means of analysis. In short, it is absurd to attempt to teach the sciences to children under twelve."

They should, up to that age, be led to Nature only for the picturesque and for poetry. Later, science may be taught them as he for example taught geometry. He said this was one of the sets of laws by which God had made and controlled the universe, and he silenced impatience in a boy who was fretting over geometry by reminding him that he was studying the Creator's mind.

Bronson did not attempt to teach natural sciences, but Miss Peabody called attention to the fact that he gave his pupils what proved to be of highest value to scientific education, in giving them the habit of weighing the meaning and considering the comparative force of words. A long preparation of this kind for the study of sciences was fully made up in the care, she thought, with which any science is mastered by a previous knowledge of words.

Bronson believed that self-analysis and the study of the "truth of our nature" in Jesus Christ were no less beneficial in the purely intellectual than in the moral education. The consideration, he said, of the true principles and conduct of life is most favorable to the development of right judgment, especially when parallel lives showing approximation to the ideal or even wanderings from it are given in connection with the study of the life of Jesus, thus affording variety of illustrations.

"Indeed, there is something peculiarly appropriate to the young in the study of Biography. But there is very little Biography published which gives an insight into the mind and especially into its formation. It is only occasionally that we find a philosopher who can read other men's experiences and to whom the incidents of a life are transparent. But for the purposes of education there should be biographies of the childhood of genius and nature, on the plan of Carlyle's 'Life of Schiller', and his articles on Burns and others."

To supply the want of biographies, Bronson relied a good deal on journal writing, which is autobiography. And while he "presented this exercise as a means to self-analysis, self-inspection and self-knowledge, — enabling the writers to give unity to their own beings by bringing all outward facts into some relation to their individuality and gathering fragments which otherwise would be lost, — they also are being assisted in the art of composition in a way the rules of rhetoric do

not do. Every one knows that merely technical knowledge of words gives very little command of language; while a rich consciousness, a quick imagination and force of feeling seem to unlock the treasury. And even so vulgar a passion as anger induces eloquence and quickens perception to the slightest innuendo. Self-analysis, biography and journal writing, therefore, since they bear upon the skilfull use of language are as truly the initiation of intellectual as of moral education."

CHAPTER X

The Little Women

AFTER the lean and thwarted years, Bronson was extraordinarily happy, in his simple, gentle way. He suddenly became a famous and favorite personage in Boston. The Boston papers commented constantly and enthusiastically on his work. Mr. Emerson, who was at that time far less famous than Bronson, gave unstintedly of his praise. Harriet Martineau announced her intention of putting the school into her forthcoming book on America.

Bronson's leaning toward mysticism which shows so clearly in his teachings was bringing him in contact with the Transcendental group in Boston, of which he shortly became the acknowledged leader. Their home constantly was thronged with people who were soon to be, if not then, the intellectual leaders of America, all of them drawing heavily on the brilliant mind and conversation of Bronson Alcott.

All this did not infringe on the nursery life of

little Anna and Louisa. Abba, whose health was not good, irked by the social duties brought upon her by the sudden growth in importance of the school, and overburdened by the problems of running the home, the children and the business end of the school, gladly left much of the training of their two children to Bronson who was, as he and she both naïvely admitted, so much better fitted for the task than she. Brilliant, impatient, high-tempered, tender — Abba's temperament was too undisciplined to lend itself readily to the disciplining of children. Bronson wrote of this in his diary.

I believe that I understand their peculiar dispositions, their tempers, the predominating associations of their minds better than their mother, and that it behooves me from a sense of duty to devote every moment not appropriated to the necessary duties of my profession to their supervision and culture.

And Bronson carried out this "behooving" to the letter. He woke at dawn with the children, dressed them for the day, superintended their before-breakfast play, and took Anna off to school with him at nine o'clock. Returning at one, after the midday dinner and after Louisa had wakened from her nap, the children were ordinarily with him in study or nursery, or walking with him on the Common until bedtime.

Conning those hundreds of pages of faded brown handwriting of ninety years ago, one becomes familiar with that quiet Boston household, for Bronson paints picture after picture: the study with its glowing coal grate and its great desk and bookcases; the staircase which led to the nursery and to "our chamber opening from it, for we want the children never to feel that we have left them alone and in the dark"; the nursery with its simple toys and Abba sitting beside the grate at her interminable sewing and mending, a critical, half-tender eye on Bronson and the two little girls; Louisa at her favorite task of moving with much puffing and blowing *all* the toys down into the study to be with father, then with equal puffing moving them *all* up the stairs again to be in the nursery with her mother.

One sees Bronson's fine blond head bent above his desk at one moment, and lifted the next to give attention to a sudden infantile riot in the nursery above; sees him stride up the stairs and enter the nursery in time to take from Louisa the poker with which she is attacking the gentle older

147

sister and see him, his quiet voice none the less severe, stay Anna's tears and Louisa's roars of wrath with a glance and a word.

There is Abba at the piano in the winter twilight, improvising delightful dance tunes to which Louisa fits strange dance steps that enthrall Bronson's sense of the mystic. And there is Anna shedding bitter tears because she is not allowed to take off her flannel undershirt on a night of zero temperature, and Louisa holding an apple in her hand which she has stolen from her father. Bronson tells the story quite perfectly:

"No! No! Me will not steal father's apple." She replaces the apple on the wardrobe shelf and then returns to it again and again, unconscious of her mother's watchful eye, and also finally succumbs to the terrible temptation. "Me cannot help it; me must have it." A little later she is standing with the core in her hand, confessing the crime to her father, a baby criminal of three.

No detail of their little lives was too small to interest Bronson, no task too menial for him to perform for them. For every fact connected with them led back in his mind to their divine origin.

Dec. 1835. I had an interesting conversation with Anna today, growing out of an attempt to

148

personate the forms of the letters by positions of the body. She was much amused by this. I put myself in various positions, representing all the letters she knew. She joined with me. We had I, proud and egotistical, repeating as he strutted across the room, his own name with great self-importance. Then we had S, crooked and deformed, imitating the goose, saying g-s-s and X with his crossed legs and upraised arms, and O, shouting, sighing, suffering, complaining. E also was represented in posture and it was while acting this that she observed the ease with which I raised myself from the floor.

"Father, what is it makes you get up so from the floor?"

"Because," said I, "my leg is made on purpose to bend. Come and see it."

She came. I bent my leg, showed her the joint at the knee saying, "Anna, see, this looks like the ball of your cup and ball."

"So does mine!" she cried. "Father, who made my knee? O, I know! God. God is in me. He tells me when I do wrong."

Then her train of thought, varied and of subtle associations became peculiarly interesting. She swung her body from her body to its Creator, and from Him to the Spirit, including sky, earth, matter, spirit, man, God, life and death. She went from father to herself, from herself to others,

men generally, from men to God above, beyond
nature. From infinite power, immeasurable space,
she descended to herself again, and still on the
same track of the infinite amid things finite, toward
God in herself — in conscience.

Is there no spiritual life ? Is there no revelation
of the infinite ? Explain it if you can, you who
deny the dignity of our natures and find nothing
spiritual in the minds of childhood. She never
had been talked to on these subjects. What she
said was not external revelation, repeated from
hearsay.

Jan. 12, 1836. Louisa's force and temerity of
will broke out in more than usual strength and
continuance today. She has formed the habit
of teasing her mother to take her and persists in
the entreaty to her own great detriment. This
evening, the request was reiterated with the usual
urgency and impatience of temper. I requested
her to cease making the request for her mother
would not take her, but she persisted. I placed
her little chair by her mother's side, and invited
her to seat herself in it. She refused. I repeated
my wish. She again showed disinclination to
comply with the requisition. I told her I would
place her in the chair if she did not get in herself.
She refused, saying, "No! No!" with her usual
force of expression, raising her tones and giving me
to understand that the decision was made in her

STEPHENS COLLEGE
LIBRARY

mind. I placed her in the chair notwithstanding her struggles. Her cries were heightened and her resistance more pronounced.

I told her she must stop crying or I would punish her — hurt her, for she must "mind father." "No! No!" she exclaimed with more decided vehemence than before. I said "Father must spank Louisa if she does not do as he says. Will she?" "No! No! Sit with mother."

I spanked her. She cried the louder. I repeated the punishment but did not obtain peace and quiet for her until I had repeated it for the third time. She then became quiet and sat in her chair talking peacefully with her mother and me until her supper was brought in.

Obedience never has been enforced on her against her determination in her mother's discipline. The consequence is that her volitions are vehement and unyielding. She resists with all her might.

I do not believe in corporal punishment except as a corrective for deep seated habits. Frowardness is, usually a misguided, misdirected tendency of the will, a force that acknowledges no superior agency, and bent on indulgence. It is a perversion of the sentiment of freedom, an overweening trust of the child in its own powers. Where vigilant and faithful supervision to the melioration of the temper and will, where a prospective and preventive discipline is pursued, little perhaps no physical suffering is needed to subdue the young spirit and bring it under parental authority. I do not believe in its efficacy except as a corrective discipline. Had the children been under my supervision continually, had the principle of prevention been carried out in the nursery, I do not believe it would have been necessary to resort to such methods. I have punished Anna so but seldom, not more than a dozen times since her birth perhaps. She is more docile than Louisa, but this arises from greater timidity of disposition as well as to greater faith and affection.

Jan. 18, 1836. I had an interesting interview with Anna at twilight, the hour when my own mind is most self reposing and when amid the blendings of light and shadow by the glowing grate of coals, e'er the lamp is lighted, the imagination shapes outward things to its own ideals. Anna seems to partake of the same mental congeniality. She is more social, vivid, shaping at that hour than any other. I often indulge her by super-adding to the outward scenery shapes for the affections, ideas for the intellect, notions for the understanding. She was sitting in her little chair where she had spent the day with her sprained ankle and asked to come and sit with me. I assisted her to come and took her on my knee. She listened to what I was saying, and after I had finished, putting her arms around me, she said, "I like you!" repeating the caress with a great show of feeling. The scenery, the blended lights and shades of twilight, the glowing fire. . .

I sit down to make some remarks on the lives and circumstances of my children but e'er I am aware, I have left the consideration of them as individuals and have merged their separate existences into the common life of the spirit. I have left their terrestrial life with the varied phenomena that typify its action and am roaming at large over the domain of the celestial world, beholding not only these, my children, in the gladsome existence there; but also, the innumerable children of the Infinite Parent Himself, the common Father.

And thus, preparing the track of the young spirit on its return to heaven, should the mind of the parent ascend to the throne of the *I Am* whence came the life and being of his child and to which it struggles mid the bewilderments and clogs of flesh again to re-ascend. Without this connexion of thought he can neither understand nor can he perform his duty as parent. He cannot appreciate the being of his child. He cannot minister to wants of which he is not conscious. He has no theory to guide his practice. He who beholds his child not only as the heir but as the present possessor of immortality will strive to open the way from his spirit for the celestial energies that are there enfolded and shape them into forms of beauty and excellence. He will be careful not to pollute its divine purity.

And thus would I regard the little ones entrusted to me for discipline and culture.

Feb. 1, 1836. Anna had a comfortless weary night. She had taken cold at school, her foot pains her, dreams troubled her mind. Her mother rose with her, bathed her foot, made her a doll and gave her as much attention as she could — The two children passed the day with their mother, Anna confined by her foot which seems much worse from the cold taken yesterday, Louisa having her sister more under her power from her perfect helplessness. Anna seemed to fear her sister's approaches and so alarming has she become to her that some discipline will be necessary to reduce Louisa to tameness. She seems practically the law of might. The stronger and bolder has the mastery over the weaker and more timid. She is still undisciplined: subject to her instinct, pursuing her purposes by any means that will lead to their attainment; Anna suffers a good deal from this temper of her sister's. She wears the mark of her sister's hand at present on her cheek!

Louisa wants animal food whereas Anna prefers vegetable. I am not sure but that Louisa's untamable spirit derives something of its ferocity from the nature of her diet. Children doubtless suffer greatly from inattention by parents to the aliment on which they are fed.

April 4, 1836. Anna's pictures are some of them very fine execution in the truest and happiest style of the art. I subjoin one as a specimen of the manner in which cuts intended for the age of children should be executed. It is taken from a series of works published in London by Baldwin and Chadwick, whose books have no representation in our country — called The Daisy, The Cowslip and Rose Bud. Anna has them all.

May 12, 1836. Louisa is a guideless creature, the child of instinct yet unenlightened by love. On the impetuous stream of instinct she has set sail and regardless alike of the quicksand and the rocks, of the careering winds and winter currents that oppose her course, she looks only toward the objects of her desires and steers proudly, adventurously, and yet without compass or chart save the gale and gleaming stars of her own will, toward the heaven of her hopes. The stronger the opposing gale, the more sullenly and obstinately does she ply her energies and when compelled to yield, she yields but to await the calming of the angry waters that she may ride on again toward her end. Richly freighted and heavy-laden is her spirit but it plays too safely with the lifting waves and exults in its own unbridled strength ; uncurbed, untaught, unguided by the skill of this life's voyagers. Experience will teach her in due time, if she have the true helmsman to guide and protect her, the secret of her strength and the way to avail herself of its potency.

Anna is already an observant voyager on the seas of time, and she rides serenely over its waves. Though apprehensive of danger and timid in venturing in the untried ways that lead to the haven of desire. Rough gales endanger her course. She has to ride on smooth and tranquil seas, and at the end she beholds the Blessed Country of the Ideal.

There is a tide in the Spirit's current that is ever setting back to the Ocean from whence it first ran.

I found at the book store some very appropriate little books for them. They were published in Philadelphia in 1824. The cuts are better than those usually given in children's books and are *colored*. The works were written by Dr. Gregory and are entitled, 1. My Father. 2. My Mother. 3. My Sister. There are several others. The furniture of the nursery will not be complete until such a series of works shall be placed within it for the inspiration of the young. I was much interested in the intensity and abstraction of thought awakened in Louisa's mind from the inspection of these pictures. Seated in her little chair, she spent a half hour on them.

Today I bought them each a little rocking chair to render their associations with regards to sitting more agreeable — Could we see the little chairs in which we once sat, might not some of the ideas associated with them in infancy and childhood be revived in our spirits and some memories of our young lives visit us again? A little chair is no unpoetic, uninspiring object, belong to whom it may. But when it is ours, the one in which our first thoughts and sentiments began to breed, how full of meaning must it be!

Louisa's spirit seems to limit its labors in self-control to short periods. During the last few days, the fit of persistence has been on her. She refuses and that obstinately whatever opposes her inclination. Her violence is at times alarming. Father, mother, sister, objects all are equally defied, and not infrequently the menace terminates in blows. Anna actually needs *protection*. Sitting with me today Louisa held my hand in hers, and while enjoying the sense of bodily contact, she seemed to be instinctively tempted to pinch me.

Anna is apt to theorize both for herself and Louisa. Louisa, intent solely on practice, is constantly demolishing Anna's air castles and irritating her spirit with a Gothic rudeness. Anna seldom provokes her sister intentionally and seems sorry when she does. Whereas, Louisa, from the mere love of action, often assaults her sister and

looks on to see what will be the result of her temerity. Instances are not infrequent when the
older flies to her mother for protection from the
wild and querulous actions of the younger !

Louisa has seemed rather unwell today. She
had a severe fall the other day which hurt her
head a little. She is very lively, however, and
thrives beyond all my expectations. She is a perfect picture of luxuriant childhood — Hers is the
wild exuberance of a powerful nature — Here is
a deep and affluent nature. A peculiar discipline
mingling severity with kindness is required to
bring out and fit in array all its powers.

Louisa's form discloses itself in beautiful pro-
portions. Her physical being seems modeled on
a dignified and imposing type : and the characteristic traits of her spirit, so far as revealed to observation, partake of a similar boldness and ampli-
tude. Powerful elements seem to be combined in
her being. She is fortunate in having her sister
as an example. Anna's profound intelligence, the
delicacy of her sentiment, the depth of her
thoughts, her meditation and ideal imagination
are all influences for Louisa's benefit.

June, 1837. The temper depends not a little on
the physical being. This forms the instrument
by which the soul manifests itself. Ill health in
infancy entails as almost necessary consequence,

indolence of will and extreme susceptibility of sentiment. And so on the other hand, a high flow
of animal nature during childhood impresses on
the soul the opposite trait of ferocity, ungovern-
able energy and passionate obstinacy.

The tendency of Anna's constitution is toward
the first of these extremes, Louisa inclines to the
latter. Both have good elements for the base of
the soul. In Anna, the soul of the meditative
genius, in Louisa, understanding, the force that
actuates the movement of the outward life, pre-
dominates. The speculative and the actual. The
ideal and the real. The spirit that conceives and
the force that executes are represented in their
natures. What Anna lacks in practical skill is
represented fully in Louisa. And Louisa's force
and hardihood of will are finely contrasted by
Anna's delicacy and depth of sentiment. Their
destiny is, of course, diverse. And they require
a different discipline. Love, kindness, with little
vigor of reproof unfold Anna's nature in the happiest way. But Louisa needs more decided meas-
ures to check the stormy current of her being.
Authority alone controls the sturdy temper of her
spirit and causes obedience. Her nature opposes
more vigorous forces to the world. Anna bears
and forebears to gain strength, growth, life.
Louisa wrestles with the obstacles and learns by
the contention. Anna will make great progress in

self knowledge by submitting to the pressure of external life. Louisa will grow strong in the knowledge of *things* by the contentions to which she dooms herself. The spirits of both have a wide field for action. Let me fit them both for the drama on which they have entered.

June, 1837. Anna was very happy at school today. She with other little ones of her age, take much interest in the readings from Miss Edge-worth's "Frank." These readings I regard as a most valuable source of instruction in self knowl-edge and the principles of conduct. Anna's pre-vious culture prepares her for this tuition. And the readiness with which she apprehends an idea or a principle is most gratifying proof of the good effects arising from the course of discipline to which she has been subjected. She appears favorably when compared with other children of her years. Her attainments are of an internal character. In acquirements she is behind many. She hardly knows the alphabet. Her ideas of numbers are undefined. But her mind is active, her imagina-tion is formative and her fancy fresh.

The children passed the afternoon with their mother. Being ill, I reclined in the chamber near and could overhear their operations. Anna was much irritated by Louisa's inter-meddling with her toys and Louisa annoyed by Anna's frequent complaints.

STEPHENS COLLEGE
LIBRARY

ANNA

Anna's extreme susceptibility is rendered more acute by want of entire sympathy between her and her mother. Of somewhat different dispositions, the mother does not comprehend Anna's wants, neither does she seize the happiest moment or the best means of allaying them — Anna asks her many questions, answers to which are of the greatest importance to her happiness and yet her mother from want of comprehension of the turn of Anna's ideas or from the deep absorption of her mind in domestic concerns cannot think it a matter of much importance to answer them, and so Anna is thrown back on her sensitive nature and seeks relief in tears or in silence. Or when the question is responded to by the mother, the answer is oftentimes too vague to be satisfactory and not doubting the ability of her mother to vouchsafe a satisfactory reply, Anna repeats the question in a tone of impatient entreaty until the mother, irritated by the repetition, replies in a similar tone, setting down the young questioner as a querulous, captious spirit and deigns no further reply. This is unfortunate as it operates against both, increases Anna's susceptibility and disturbs her mother's repose.

With Louisa, the mother has more sympathy. She comprehends her mind more fully and is, of course, more fully master of its associations. They are more alike.

It seems hardly possible that any one could have come so near accurate prophecy of the future of two children scarcely out of babyhood as Bronson did in these early diaries. And yet Louisa's own diary, published a generation later, corroborates all of her father's estimate of her forceful, tempestuous nature and of her dramatic talents.

CHAPTER XI

Conversations on the Gospels

THE farther Bronson penetrated into children's minds, the more firmly persuaded he became that talking to them and allowing them to talk about Jesus Christ was a supremely good method of leading them to an understanding of Spirit. He had not been conducting the Temple School for a year before he began to arrange the four gospels into a continued story which he told to the children, at frequent intervals. He did not wish the children to think the meaning of the Scripture was a matter of authority. He allowed them to make their own interpretations and attempted to guard them from actual mistakes only by the general influence of his moral and intellectual discipline.

Nothing in the school curriculum so intrigued the children's interest as did these conversations on the Gospels. Observing this, Miss Peabody began making a separate record of them. The children's interest finally reached the point where some of them asked for Sunday hours on the subject. Bronson was greatly pleased. His educational dreams were broadening day by day and this opened the way to the realization, he thought, of one of the biggest of them.

He says of this:

Dec. 15, 1835. I met some of my pupils, this morning, for the second time. Though the snow was deep and the morning unpleasant, I was gratified at finding so many present with some of their friends. This beginning of my Sunday readings is encouraging: I trust the interest excited at the beginning will not die away by time and repetition. I see in this little assemblage the germ of a Church that shall bring not only the young but adults (parents and others) to hear the simple words of the Gospel, and find something in them suited to their spiritual growth and joy.

Successful preaching implies the utterance of the profoundest truth in simple phrases, touching the common sense of everyone, the child or the adult. In our language there are simple, universal, living terms (understood alike by the sage and the child, by every unsophisticated being) for the representation of the common wants and supplies of our spiritual life. To find these terms and use them in their living sense is the art of the instructor.

I am to teach — and I am to teach that which

is of universal import — the common nature we inherit. I shall illustrate this first to the young mind : in the faith that as I succeed in unfolding the deep things of our being to the sense of childhood, I shall clear the vision of the grown man to his own state and the means of renovation. I shall hold up the mirror of childhood to the view of adolescence, that it may see the presence of the Infinite and sinless One. A church, when it shall come, will give me full scope.

Unshackled by the time-worn forms and ceremonies that cramp and stupefy the mind in the discharge of worship; having young and unbeguiled spirits whose sense is clear, whose instincts alive : and having no predecessor whose forms can hamper my movements, — I can go on in the true spirit of induction, finding what is wanted by consulting the laws of the young mind.

I trust that I shall unfold some of the essential grounds and conditions of man's spiritual being, shall popularize a true sense of human nature, and turn men's minds to the culture of childhood as the primary duty. I seek to be simple and to have docility, to apprehend what God sendeth to my apprehension, and to labor and love for the sake of labor and living.

So for something over a year, Bronson and his pupils carried on their extraordinary conversations.

It is important to remember that only two of

the children were twelve years of age. All the others were ten or under. Josiah, who talked the best of all, although he stammered, was only six. Little Emma was seven, Augustine was eight, and one must remember that these conversations took place at a time when the universal belief was that human beings were born in sin and were doomed to perdition unless "saved." Miss Peabody, Miss Margaret Fuller, Mrs. Hawthorne, took down the children's words exactly. There is space here to give only portions of each day's conversations and one is fearful lest in not giving the whole that the remarkable beauty and sweetness of the whole may be lost.

Bronson began Jan. 5, 1836, by reading them the account of Zacharias' vision in Luke I. 1–57.

ALEXANDER   I don't see why the angel made him dumb except he did not want Zacharias to tell the people he was going to have a child.

GEORGE   I don't think Zacharias was wrong in not believing the angel on the angel's own record. God might have convinced Zacharias that it was a good angel. It's not always wrong to doubt. Zacharias could not perhaps believe such good news because he might have always thought he was not good enough to have a child. Very good people often think they are worse than they really are.

EDWARD B.   God made him dumb not to punish him but to give him an idea of God's power and convince him that God could make old people have children or do anything.

MR. ALCOTT   But why should not old people have children?

LUCIA   Because they would not live long enough to bring them up.

CHARLES   I suppose Zacharias thought so much about the little baby that it came, even when he was old.

ANDREW   John's having the Holy Ghost means that when he grew up he would not give up to his body.

WILLIAM   If *we* could see God we'd never do wrong.

LUCIA   When John was first born, his mother did not know it, for he was born in the night. But she

167

found him by her side in the night. All babies are born at night.

CHARLES   Elizabeth must have had some vision as well as Zacharias or how would she know the child was there? Zacharias could not speak.

LUCIA   Why are most children born in the night?

MR. ALCOTT   Children do come in the night very frequently. God draws a veil over these sacred events and they ought never be thought of except with reverence. The coming of a spirit is a great event. It should free us from all wrong thoughts. All birth is as sacred as that of John or Christ's. — Why was Jesus called the Son of God?

EDWARD   Because he was like God.

LUCIA   Because he was descended from heaven.

JOSIAH   Because he was a part of God's soul. He was God's voice on earth. He was born of God's power.

168

MR. ALCOTT — Who of you think that the spirit, the power of God was acting when your spirit was beginning?
(*all rise*)

MR. ALCOTT — Who of you think that when your fathers and mothers loved each other and wanted a child of their own to love, God was present and gave a spirit from himself in answer to this prayer?
(*all rise*)

MR. ALCOTT — You may give me some emblems of birth.

ALEXANDER — Birth is like rain. It comes from heaven.

LUCIA — I think it is like a small stream coming from a great sea. It becomes larger and larger until at last it is large enough to send out other streams.

SAMUEL — Birth is like the rising light of the sun. The setting is death.

ANDREW — God's wind came upon the ocean of life and washed up the waters a little into a channel and that is birth. They run up farther, and that is living.

MR. ALCOTT   There is no adequate emblem of birth in the external world except the physical facts that attend it with which you are not acquainted and they are only the sign of the bodily birth. You have seen the rose opening from the seed with the help of the atmosphere. This is the birth of the rose. It typifies the bringing forth of the spirit by pain, labor, and patience. Why did Mary feel such joy in the birth of her child?

LUCIA   Because she knew he was going to be a great man. I think she and Elizabeth must have had a very pleasant time talking about what their sons would be.

JOSIAH   *All* mothers think their sons will be great.

EMMA   Yes, but our mothers did n't have angels appear to them.

CHARLES   If such a great event was to come again, God would make just the same arrangements as he did for Jesus. No angel appeared to my mother, but perhaps the same thoughts came to her.

170

WELLES   I have not yet found out whether angels come in bodies or not.

MR. ALCOTT   Was it an angel that appeared to Mary's eyes?

ANDREW   No. Mary saw the angel with her spirit. It was her imagination gave it shape.

LUCIA   What joy she must have felt!

MR. ALCOTT   What do you feel when you feel joy? Where does it come from?

CHARLES   From the heart — from the spirit.

MR. ALCOTT   What is meant by the word quicken?

CHARLES   Enliven. You say quickening ray.

MR. ALCOTT   And we say the quick and the dead. Jesus quickened men. Joy quickens the heart. When Mary's salutation sounded on Elizabeth's ear, she felt that the child promised was hers. It was quickened into being. This always takes place sometime before a child is born. The heart then thus filled with life and joy is said to be quickened. Mothers feel this when they know children are to be given to them. The angel

171

of love first tells a mother a child is coming. Sometimes she has other signs. Who now will give me a picture of the scene in Bethlehem when Jesus was born?

Here followed charming word paintings by the children of the immortal picture. Afterward Lucia said:

It must have been bliss for Mary.

MR. ALCOTT　　Did you ever hear the lines, "The throe of suffering is the birth of bliss"?

GEORGE　　Yes. It means that love and joy and faith lead you to suffering which makes more happiness for you.

MR. ALCOTT　　Yes, you have the thought. And a mother suffers when she has her child — When she is going to have her child, she gives up her body to God and he works on it in a mysterious way and brings forth the child's spirit in a little body of its own and when it comes, she is blissful.

CHARLES　　I think it ought to be the father. He is so much stronger.

172

MR. ALCOTT	He suffers because he sees the suffering without power to relieve it. — You must think of your body as the spirit made visible, a part of God's spirit, just as Christ's was, and hold it sacred.
EMMA	How beautiful it would be on earth if no one ever did wrong.
WELLES	If it had not been for Adam —
MR. ALCOTT	If it had not been for Welles — and for Mr. Alcott — and for all imperfect human creatures —
JOSIAH	There would be no pain.
MR. ALCOTT	What is pain for?
EMMA	To make us patient.
MR. ALCOTT	What word that includes patience in its meaning betokens a mind above all trouble?
CHARLES	A word meaning, without passion.
MR. ALCOTT	Yes, a word that describes an attribute that God has. Only think of God getting in a passion!
NATHAN	God would not be God if he got in a passion.
MR. ALCOTT	Are you like God when you do?
FRANCIS	Not in the least like God.

MR. ALCOTT   I'll tell you the word I mean — repose. People who have repose are less troubled about outward things. They look down upon the world as God does. The greatest souls are full of repose.

SAMUEL   Jesus meant to teach us not to mind the body's pain.

CHARLES   Pain is of small consequence when the body is hurt to make the soul better.

MR. ALCOTT   Everyone is a visitor on earth from God. I hope you will all be pleasant visitors and not find fault. Do you think a drunkard is a pleasant visitor? (*They all laugh.*)

EMMA   I'm not a very pleasant visitor, but I'm having a very pleasant visit.

Jan. 10, 1836, Mr. Alcott read "The Purification of the Temple." John II, 13–17, and explained the origin of the Feast, the Courts of the Temple, and asked the children what the story meant to them.

JOSIAH
(aged 6)   Jesus meant to show them that they were wicked in making any

place to Worship God in, a place for anything else. I can see Jesus going into the Temple and the little tables of shops and sheep lying about. Jesus was smiling when he went in but when he sees this, he looks pretty cross.

EMMA   It was indignation.   Anger wants to hurt, to injure, but indignation only feels wrong and wants others to feel so too.

MR. ALCOTT   Is the outward expression of the two alike?

EMMA   No, when indignant, one looks resolute.

ELLEN   I think it was a sorrowful look in Jesus.

EMMA   Yes, there is sorrow in indignation.

FREDERIC   He felt displeasure: there was no anger nor peevishness nor fretfulness.   He seemed rather impatient, but not worrisome; he wanted to get them away, quick.

FRANKLIN   I have felt he cried a little.

FREDERIC   But he did not use the whip.

MR. ALCOTT   What was the whip for?

175

SAMUEL   It was the emblem of warning, of chastisement.

MR. ALCOTT   What made them all go out of the Temple if he did not use the whip?

JOSIAH   He took the whip to drive the cattle out.

MR. ALCOTT   What made the people go out?

JOSIAH   Because they were afraid he would whip them. He could not have intended for one moment to whip them.

JOHN B.   I think he whipped them but very calmly without passion, so as to make them think.

Mr. Alcott then read of the Wisdom of Jesus, John II. 23–5 and then asked, "How did Jesus know what was in man?"

JOSIAH   He was good and got what he knew from God, just as I do.

MR. ALCOTT   Does God give you all the knowledge you try after?

JOSIAH   Yes, and he gave me one thing I did not try after, and that is my Spirit and he put it in my body. My body could not go to God and try after a spirit.

MR. ALCOTT	Can your spirit carry your body to God ?
JOSIAH	No, my body cannot be carried to God. Only spirits can go to God.
MR. ALCOTT	Who made Jesus Christ ?
SAMUEL R.	No one made his spirit.
FRANKLIN	Jesus always was.
JOSEPH	Jesus must have found out what was in man by a miracle for he could not have found it out the way people find out other things.
MR. ALCOTT	Where was the miracle ?
JOSEPH	In his mind, he was so much better than we are.
MR. ALCOTT	If you were very good, would there be miracles in your mind ?
JOSEPH	If I were as good as he. There never was a miracle in my mind, but I should like to have one.
MR. ALCOTT	When did Jesus get his knowledge ?
MARTHA	He went into his own soul.
JOHN B.	Jesus knew what was in man because God told him.
MR. ALCOTT	In a different way from what he tells you ?

JOHN B.	No, but Jesus was better and God told him more.
MR. ALCOTT	Does God telling depend on you or God? If you were as willing and eager to be taught by God as Jesus was, would you know as much? Is the knowledge ready for you?
JOHN B.	Yes, but God gave Jesus more power than he gave me.
MR. ALCOTT	Whether he tried or not?
JOHN B.	No. It does not depend on trying.
MR. ALCOTT	May we say there is a Christ in the depths of our Spirit which may be brought out of us if we try as Jesus did?
AUGUSTINE	No: because Jesus was God and we cannot be said to have God in us.
FREDERIC	I do not think Jesus Christ himself is in my Spirit but only powers equal to his. . . .

February 1836. Mr. Alcott read the conversations of Jesus with the woman of Samaria. John IV, 1–30.

MR. ALCOTT	What interested you most?
JOSEPH	The living water. It means spiritual water.
MR. ALCOTT	What do you mean by spiritual water?
JOSEPH	I cannot express it — it is truth.
JOSIAH	Jesus meant to tell her he would give her truth.
MR. ALCOTT	Did the woman understand?
FRANKLIN	No, she thought of water for the body.
EDWARD	You know, she asked him what he was going to draw with and that shows she thought it was some common sort of stream he spoke of.
CHARLES	He told her that if she knew who it was speaking to her, she would also know what he meant.
MR. ALCOTT	How would she know?
CHARLES	Because if she knew his nature she would know his spoken emblems.
W. AUGUSTUS	He meant he could make her better. She did not understand but I don't think it was wrong

for she never had been taught about figures of speech. I have a living spring in my Spirit if my passions don't dry it up.

MR. ALCOTT   You have seen a stagnant pool: a bad effluvia rises from it: a green substance collects on the surface: disagreeable reptiles gather round it. Why is this?

W. AUGUSTUS   Because no living water comes to it.

MR. ALCOTT   What is such a place an emblem of?

W. AUGUSTUS   A self-indulgent, bad person.

EDWARD J.   Beautiful flowers sometimes grow around stagnant waters.

MR. ALCOTT   That is true: and bad people do good and beautiful things, sometimes. Some of the Spirit given them at first is not yet quenched. Name some spiritual waters.

LEMMUEL   Love, faith, generosity, hope, truth.

MR. ALCOTT   Do you always drink that last water?

LEMMUEL   (*Blushing*) No.

180

ANDREW	reading, "And the water that I shall give thee shall be a well of water, springing up into everlasting life." The water is spirit. Spirit makes goodness. Goodness lasts always.
MR. ALCOTT	Why does not the body last always?
ANDREW	Because it is no part of God, but is a part of the earth. The spirit is a part of God.
MARTHA	Living water means holiness. God sends it in.
MR. ALCOTT	Where does he get it from?
MARTHA	From himself.
MR. ALCOTT	Does it get spoilt in us?
MARTHA	Yes, till he fixes it again.
EDMUND C.	I was interested in Jesus being weary and sitting by the well.
JOHN B.	All the waters in me are spoiled.
SAMUEL T.	I was most interested in this verse, "He that drinks of this water shall thirst again, but he that shall drink of the water that I shall give him shall never thirst." He meant by this that

	those who heard what he taught and did it, should live always, should never die, their spirits should never die.
MR. ALCOTT	Can a spirit die at any rate?
SAMUEL T.	For a spirit to die is to leave off being good.
ELLEN	I was interested in these words, "Ye worship ye know not what." The Samaritans worshipped idols and there was no meaning to that. She thought the place of worship was more important than the place itself. That's why Jesus said, "Woman, the hour is coming and now is, when neither in this mountain, —"
JOSIAH	I was interested most in this verse, "God is a spirit and they that worship him must worship him in spirit and in truth." It means that to feel our prayers is more important than to say the words.
LEMMUEL	And when we pray, and pray sincerely.
MR. ALCOTT	What is praying sincerely?

LEMMUEL	Praying the truth.
MR. ALCOTT	What is to be done in praying truth? When you think of prayer, do you think of a posture of the body — of words?
LEMMUEL	(*earnestly*) I think of something else, but I cannot express it.
MR. ALCOTT	Josiah is holding up his hand. Can he express it?
JOSIAH	(*bursts out*) To pray, Mr. Alcott, is to be good, really. There must be something outward about prayer, but we must have some words sometimes, sometimes we need not. If we don't feel the prayer it is worse than never to have said a word of prayer. It is wrong not to pray, but it is much more wrong to speak prayers and not to pray. We had better do nothing about it, Mr. Alcott. We must feel the words we pray and we must do what belongs to the words. . . .

A long discussion followed among the children on responsive and formal prayer forms. Josiah held the floor so frequently that Mr. Alcott quieted him and asked some one else to tell him where and how to pray.

GEORGE K.	Place is of no consequence. Christian prayed in the cave of Giant Despair. We can pray anywhere because we have faith anywhere.
ELLEN	I heard a woman say once that she could pray best when she was at work; that when she was scouring the floor, she could ask God to cleanse her mind.
MR. ALCOTT	Faith, then is necessary?
GEORGE K.	Yes, for it is faith that makes the prayer.
MR. ALCOTT	I will now vary the question. Is there any prayer in Patience?
ALL	A great deal.
MR. ALCOTT	In Doubt?
GEORGE K.	No, but in Faith.
MR. ALCOTT	In Laziness?
ALL BUT JOSIAH	No.
JOSIAH	I should think that Laziness was the prayer of the body, Mr. Alcott.

184

MR. ALCOTT   Yes, I should think so. The body tries to be still more body. It tries to get down into the clay. It tries to sink but the spirit is always trying to make it do something.

EDWARD J.   Lazy people sometimes have passions that make them act.

Mr. Alcott talked then on the idea of living God with the heart, mind, soul, and the kind of Devotion it expressed. Thus he asked the question:

"Do you feel that Conscience is stronger than the mountain? Can you say to yourself, I can remove this mountain?"

JOSIAH   (*Bursts out*) Yes, Mr. Alcott! I do not mean that with my body I can lift up a mountain — with my hand. But I can feel. And I know that my Conscience is greater than the mountain for it can feel and do and the mountain cannot. It was made and that is all. But my Conscience can grow. It is the same kind of Spirit that made the mountain be in the first place. I do not know what it may be and do.

The Body is a mountain and the Spirit says, be moved, and it is moved into another place. . . .

MR. ALCOTT   Yes, Josiah, that is all true and we are glad to hear it. Shall someone else speak now, beside you?

JOSIAH   Oh, Mr. Alcott! Then I will stay in at recess and talk.

MR. ALCOTT   When a little infant opens its eyes upon this world and sees things out of itself and has the feeling of admiration is there in that feeling the beginning of worship?

JOSIAH   No, Mr. Alcott. A little baby does not worship. It opens its eyes upon the outward world and sees things and perhaps wonders what they are, but it does n't know anything about worship or about itself. There is no worship in it. It must have temptation, I think, before it can know the meaning of worship.

MR. ALCOTT   But is not there a feeling that comes up from within to answer to the things that come to the eyes and ears?

186

JOSIAH   But feeling is not worship, Mr. Alcott.

MR. ALCOTT   Can there be worship without feeling?

JOSIAH   No, but there can be feeling without worship. If I prick myself with a pin, I feel, but I do not worship.

MR. ALCOTT   That is only bodily feeling. But what I mean is that the infant finds its power to worship in the feeling that at first is only admiration of what is without.

JOSEPH   No, no. I know what surprise is and I know what admiration is, and perhaps the little creature feels that. But she does not know enough to know that she has a Conscience or that there is temptation. My little sister feels and she knows some things, but she does not worship.

"Here," writes Miss Peabody, "I was obliged to pause as I was altogether fatigued with keeping my pen in long and uncommonly constant motion and requisition. I was enabled to preserve the words better than usual because Josiah had so much of the conversation, whose impediment of

187

speech, stammering, makes his enunciation slow and whose fine choice of language and steadiness of mind make him easy to follow and remember."

Miss Margaret Fuller, Mrs. Hawthorne, Miss Peabody, all those who heard the conversations and helped to record them urged Bronson to publish them. He was a little fearful that giving the material to the public might be premature, but finally he yielded and early in 1837, the conversations on the Gospels were given to the world.

Bronson had written a characteristic introduction. "It is the record of an attempt to unfold the idea of spirit from the Consciousness of Childhood and to trace its intellectual and corporeal relations, its temptations and disciplines, its struggles and conquests while in the flesh. To this end, the character of Jesus has been presented to the consideration of children as the brightest symbol of spirit and they have been encouraged to express their views regarding it.

The Conductor of these conversations has reverently explored their consciousness for the testimony which it might furnish in favor of the truth of Christianity. It is with no little solicitude that he ventures these documents before the eyes of others. He feels that his book should be studied in simplicity. It is in no small measure the production of children. It is a record of their consciousness, a natural history of the undepraved spirit. It is the testimony of unspoiled natures to the spiritual beauty of Jesus. It is a revelation of the divinity in the soul of childhood. Like the sacred volume, of which it is indeed a juvenile commentary, of which it is an interpretation, it cannot be at once apprehended in all its bearings and find its true value.

There may be those, however, who shall avail themselves of its statements, views and speculations to the detriment of religion and humanity: not perceiving that it is a work intended rather to awaken thought, enkindle feeling, and quicken to duty, than to settle opinions, or promulgate sentiments of any kind. Whoever shall find its significance will scarce treat with disrespect these products of the sacred being of childhood.

For childhood utters sage things, worthy of all note and he who scoffs at its improvisations, or perverts its simple sayings, proves the corruption of his own being and his want of reverence for the Good, the Beautiful, the True, the Holy; he beholds not the face of the heavenly Father."

CHAPTER XII

The Crash

OTHER things beside the Temple School were happening in the Alcott family. In 1835, Elizabeth (Beth), the third daughter was born and royally welcomed. And in 1835, also, Bronson and his wife Abba visited William Lloyd Garrison in the Leverett Street Jail. Boston was at this time an ardent pro-slavery town and Garrison had dared to start violent anti-slavery agitation within the sacred shadow of Boston Common. For this he was mobbed by "gentlemen of high standing and repute", and his clothing almost torn from his body as they fastened a rope around his neck and dragged him through the streets. He was barely saved from hanging and was lodged in jail to prevent Boston from killing him.

Naturally Bronson and Abba were Abolitionists, and naturally, both being fearless, they visited Garrison, to show Boston where they stood on the slavery question.

Boston did not greatly like the gesture. But

Bronson's charm, his love for children and theirs
for him, his profound and lucid thought not only
about education but about religion, — all these
made it possible for Bronson to go farther than
any one else without censure.   But he overstepped
himself when he issued the conversations on the
Gospels.

Samuel May read the book before publication
and prophesied to Abba what actually happened.

I am sure he has struck a new vein of hidden
ore. The book I shall recommend to parents
generally. I shall ask no one to read it who will
not ponder it well. . . .   It is not to be expected
that this book will meet with a very favorable
reception. The Orthodox will scowl at it because
it shows that man is not by nature what their religion requires he should be. They will be afraid
to give it unqualified praise because it expresses
too plainly the result to which some of their prominent doctrines inevitably lead and the public
(they will think) are not prepared for such an
exposure. But I hope that the book would be read by a
sufficient number . . . to keep the great idea
which the book discloses forever before the minds
of men until it has effected some radical changes
in the theory and principles of education. Mr.
Alcott may not live to see this good done; he may

never in this world be rewarded for his pains. But he has uttered a word which will never cease to sound intelligibly to some minds and to stir them deeply.

I am grieved to hear that you have had so much to try the patience of your spirit and the strength of your body. I have feared that you might break down : but then I know that the power of endurance in women is apt to be commensurate with the demand upon her and my prayer has been and is that your strength may be equal to your trials.

Abba was financial manager of the school and the family and while the school seemed to flourish, Bronson could not be brought to press parents for the tuition. The income for the first year had been but $1,794, and for the second $1,649, and for the third, $1,395. Out of this, the teachers' salaries, the expenses of the school building and the family living had to come. And also, during the past year, a little son had been born, only to die within a few days. Abba was ill-prepared for the reception of the conversations.

Had Bronson blown up Boston Common with dynamite, he could not have so startled and amazed Boston as he did by the contents of this book. The Boston papers received it and then proceeded to attack Bronson with a ferocity

equaled only by that which they had visited on
Garrison. The *Boston Courier* suggested that he
be indicted for blasphemy, and quoted a pro-
fessor of Harvard to the effect that "one-third of
Mr. Alcott's book was absurd, one-third blasphe-
mous and one-third obscene."

The hue and cry in the papers aroused the public to an extraordinary degree and on a day in late
January, Bronson was called to the door of his
school. Jammed into the portico and filling the
street before the Temple was a mob of people,
ministers, teachers, parents of his pupils, intel-
lectuals-in-fact and intellectual-riffraff. Bronson
closed the doors behind him and stood before
them, bareheaded in the bitter cold, beautiful head
uplifted, nostrils dilated, a gentleman unafraid.

"Close the school!" shouted the mob.

"Give us our children!"

"Retract that devilish book! Bring out all
your copies and burn them!"

"Close the school! Dismiss the children and
hand over the key."

"No," replied Bronson quietly. "I cannot do
that."

The foremost of the mob lunged forward and
laid hands on him. The gentleness suddenly left

Bronson's lips. Something steel hard appeared in his blue eyes.

"You will disperse at once!" His voice carried above the uproar to the entire edge of the mob.

Derisive cries met him but those who were plucking at his clothes dropped their hands. At this moment, a little door to an anteroom beside the main doors opened, and a small girl of five peered out. She was a slender little thing with a beautiful, piquant face and tempestuous dark eyes.

"Father!" she cried, "the children sent me for you!"

She ran to Bronson and he lifted her in his arms.

"Go away at once," he repeated to the mob.

The child sensed that her father was in danger and as unafraid as he, she threw her arms about his neck and lifted her little head in his own gesture of authority.

"Go away, bad people!" she ordered.

It was Louisa, appearing in public for the first time as the protector and champion of the father whom she adored.

There was something hypnotic in the dignity and calm of Bronson and his daughter Louisa. Something that persuaded the better spirits in the mob that it was acting in a ridiculous manner, and it turned tail and departed in as casual a way as it could. When the last man had left the Temple portico, Bronson carried his shivering little daughter into the schoolroom and lessons for that day proceeded as usual.

Bronson had no weapon save his own dignity for meeting these attacks, but Emerson wrote a letter to the *Courier* protesting against their unfairness. He wrote Bronson also.

Concord, March 24, 1837. My dear Friend, — I exceedingly regret the unfavorable notice of the book . . . . I hate to have all the little dogs barking at you, for you have something better to do than to attend to them : but every beast must do after its kind and why not these ? And you will hold by yourself and presently forget them. Whatever you do at school or concerning the school, pray let not the pen halt, for that must be your last and longest lever to lift the world withal. And if you would compare chapters of accidents with celebrated men, go read the paper on Mirabeau by Carlyle in the new *Westminster Review*. It is all thunder and monishes us of the might that in us lies, even in depression and under the frown of the incapable.

You are so deeply grounded in God that I shall not fear for you any loss of faith by opposition ;

but I do not want these people to shut the school for the moment. But you will bide your time and with views so large and peculiar can better afford to wait than other men. Look at my Mirabeau again.

I talked to Dr. Channing. I found him just to your character, wholly, but staggered by your opinions and, as I think, not just to your powers. I told him so . . . . I shall be in town Monday or Tuesday and mean to come and see you.

Yours affectionately, R. W. Emerson

Emerson's letter in the *Courier* protested against the picking out of a phrase or two from the text.

These phrases, innocent enough to the reader of the whole book, were copied with horror into another paper and now again have kindled the anger of your correspondent: and even your own urbanity has failed you, sir, for the moment. In behalf of this book, I have but one plea to make, namely this, that it be read. Any reasonable man will perceive that fragments out of a new theory of Christian instruction are not in the best place for examination between the Price Current and the Shipping List. Try the effect of a passage from Plato's Phaedo or the Confessions of St. Augustine in the same place.

Mr. Alcott has given the proof in the beautiful introduction to this work, as all who have read it know, of a strong mind and pure heart. A practical teacher, he has dedicated for years his rare gifts to the science of education. These Conversations contain abundant evidence of extraordinary thought either in the teacher or the pupils, or both. He aims to make children think and in every question of a moral nature to send them back on themselves for an answer. He aims to show children something holy in their own consciousness: thereby to make them really reverent and to make the New Testament a living book to them.

Mr. Alcott's methods cannot be said to have a fair trial. But he is making an experiment in which the friends of education are interested. And I ask you, sir, whether it is wise or just to add to the anxieties of his enterprise a public clamor against some detached pages of a book which as a whole is pervaded with original thoughts and sincere piety.

R. W. Emerson

Others beside Emerson were indignant. Mrs. Hawthorne wrote a letter to Bronson full of loyalty toward him and indignation toward those who had so meticulously misinterpreted his book, particularly the passages on Birth.

I could not have imagined that those conversations about Birth which I recorded would not be received with reverence and thanks by all who might have the privilege of either hearing or reading them. I felt my own mind elevated by them . . . . I heard you were quite calm amid the turmoil. I expected it and do not wonder. New ideas are always received with consternation and conventional habits of thought are like adamant around the general mind. . . . But I mourn for the library books : for it is with a most bitter pang that I heard not long since that you are about to sell your library, — that choice and beautiful library.

Yes, the library that Bronson had so painstakingly gathered was gone. People were withdrawing pupils from the school. Debts were heavy — he was carrying not only those incurred in starting the Temple School, but was carrying some old debts belonging to his father — and as soon as the first newspaper raised its voice against him, his creditors began to crowd him. Then came Harriet Martineau's book, and among other American institutions which she found suitable for ridicule was Bronson's school.

The attack was uncalled-for and unfair, showing at its very worst the bitterness of spirit that marred the famous Englishwoman's career. The book was widely read in Boston, the portion relating to Bronson much quoted, and again the school became the subject of adverse comment and bitter controversy.

Margaret Fuller took Miss Martineau to task in no uncertain terms. She wrote her a letter quite in the Englishwoman's own tart manner.

Many passages in your book are deformed by intemperance of epithet. Would your heart, could you but investigate the matter, approve such over-statement, such a crude, intemperate tirade as you have been guilty of about Mr. Alcott — a true and noble man, a philanthropist whom a true and noble woman, also a philanthropist, should have delighted to honor. He is a philoso-pher worthy of the palmy times of ancient Greece, a man whom the worldlings of Boston hold in as much honor as the worldlings of ancient Athens held Socrates. They smile to hear their verdict confirmed from the other side of the Atlantic by their censor, Harriet Martineau.

But there was no staying the war dogs. Bron-son did not know how to sway public opinion. Mentally and spiritually he was so far ahead of his contemporaries that he could only sit and endure, bewildered by their stupidity. He could not set back the clock of his mind to their half barbaric time! He could only maintain his prin-ciples and suffer, only Abba knew how much.

The school struggled on, in constantly decreasing numbers and finally, Bronson himself set the death seal on the Temple door.

All the weary months while Boston heckled him, Bronson was determinedly backing Garrison in his stand against slavery. Pro-slavery Boston added this fact to its list of grievances against the schoolmaster. One by one the children on whom Bronson had lavished the wealth of his genius were removed from the Temple, each empty little seat thrusting like a sword at his heart. Abba became ill with anxiety. Anna and Louisa felt acutely the atmosphere of hostility and ceased to thrive. Bronson wrote in his diary:

My children are suffering for want of purer air, renovating imagery and spiritual inspiration. I ought to devote this month to them. . . . They are morbid in sensibility, dimmed in intellectual vision and require the benefits of natural and spiritual sympathy to raise them from this depression. The city does not give their young natures room: they are fettered and fall back prey on sentiment, instinct, ideas, that have not been allowed to flow forth amid encroaching circumstances. . . . My income is small, inadequate to meet the claims of my family and also carry on the school. What I earn is already pledged by obligation to others

STEPHENS COLLEGE
LIBRARY

and I have already anticipated the earnings of the
next two or three years, even should I be successful. And so the claims of my family are to be set
aside for the claims of others. Thus I am bound,
perplexed.

It was in the winter of 1838 that Bronson took
into the school a little colored girl — his ultimate
gesture on the slavery question.

It took Boston several days to absorb the full
horror of this act. But when it actually entered
the consciousness of the community that this foul
deed had been perpetrated, a committee that had
all the nucleus of a mob in its virtuous indignation, burst into the schoolroom led by a matron
who had once been devoted to the Alcotts.

The handful of children were grouped in their
little chairs before Bronson. The sun shone
through the fine Gothic window on the figure of
Silence, and the little child in marble, Aspiration,
perched in the corner of Bronson's desk. The
four years of use had made the room a very sanc-
tuary for children, a holy place wherein their
spirits woke and grew.

Bronson, his face a little gaunt, for the Alcotts
ate sparingly, in these hard days, looked up as the
committee entered. There must have been twenty

men and women who came in without the formal-
ity of a knock.

The matron snatched at her own child, a boy of
ten.

"Come, Charles, I did not realize that you were
associating with black scum."

"I'm not," said Charles indignantly; "she's
not black, she's light brown, like I explained
to you. And she's not scum. She has a better
soul than any of us. She can sing like an angel. Let me go, Mother, and take these people
out of the school. We don't allow any noise in
here."

Keeping the boy's hand in hers, the mother
turned to Bronson. "I allowed him to stay for
nearly four years because he pleaded so with me.
But this is too much. A nigger!"

Her words loosed every adult tongue in the room,
save Bronson's. He stood behind his desk, a look
of puzzled wonder that gradually hardened into
indignation on his careworn face. They accused
him of fraud, of teaching their children nothing, of
keeping up appearances on borrowed money, of
stupidity, of blasphemy, of obscenity.

When Bronson had had enough he suddenly
raised his long arm and thundered, "Silence!"

and in the surprised pause that followed his gesture he said, sternly :

"Be quiet, while I question the children."
Then he turned to Charles and said gently, "Why
did you plead with your mother to stay in the
Temple school, my boy ?"

Charles lifted his chin. "Because, I never knew
I had a brain or a soul till I came to you. You
taught me what to do with them both."

"And you, Josiah," turning to the six-year old
boy whose mother was holding his hand, "what
do you think about the school ?"

Josiah, stuttering, answered in a clear treble,
"I found God here. I want to stay."

Bronson smiled at the little fellow, then spoke
to a girl of nine, "Mary, do you want to leave the
school ?"

"No ! No !" replied Mary, with a sob. "It's been
so interesting to think like you show us how, here."

And then to the little colored girl, a pretty
mulatto child with long, black curls, "Ellen, why
did you come to my school ?"

The child answered in a full, soft voice, "My
father said you would teach me how to save my
race."

There was a minute's silence after this but, after

all, the children's evidence was to avail him nothing. A man who had been standing in the background now came forward and laid a large hand on the marble figure of Aspiration. "Sorry, Mr. Alcott, but I've got to close you out here. Your creditors have turned to the law. I'm Sheriff Brown."

Louisa and Anna had crowded close to their father while he questioned the other children. When the sheriff laid his hand on the statue, Louisa left her father to push indignantly at the desecrating fingers.

"Don't touch it," she cried. "Go away! You are making my father unhappy."

"Yes, we'll go, Miss Impertinence," declared Charles' mother. "And not a living soul of us will come back."

Nor did they.

Leaving the beautiful schoolroom in the keeping of Sheriff Brown, Bronson, leading a daughter by either hand, Anna crying and Louisa's little face crimson with anger, crossed the Common and entered his home. There Abba, after one look at his face, did not need the indignant explanations of the children. She understood and took him to her loyal heart.

204

CHAPTER XIII

Soul Searching

YES, thank God that Abba understood what had happened to Bronson. She understood that the illness that overtook him was of the soul and not of the body, and she nursed him tenderly, yet in a state of loyal protest that was tonic to his grief.

"My schoolroom! My beautiful schoolroom!" says his diary. And that was the only beautiful schoolroom Bronson ever was to possess.

Abba wrote to her brother Sam.

You see how roughly they have handled my husband. He has been a quiet sufferer but none the less a sufferer because quiet. He stands to it, through it all, that this is not an ungrateful, cruel world. I rail. He reasons and consoles me as if I were the injured one. I do not know a more exemplary hero under trials than this same "visionary.". . .

It is a low state of moral discrimination that will give an honorable discharge to the man who has been twenty years gambling in fancy stocks, but drives into the region of starvation, an exalted spirit, whose desires and efforts for the best years of his life have been to elevate the moral and intellectual condition of mankind. I try not to believe it but the cruel sacrifices we are called upon daily to make compel me to despair of better things yet awhile.

Can Mr. Alcott have time to work out his problem, we may yet hide our faces and strike our breasts for shame at our incredulity. I say *ours* for I have been among his sceptics and he still thinks me almost impotent in faith. But his patient endurance staggers me. And the undaunted manner in which he assumes his burdens and cares, giving up with cheerful submission those things which I know are dear to his heart and lovely to his eye for the rigors of toil and privation, fill me with admiration. There is no sighing or complaining, but silent bowing to the dispensations of injustice and ignorance where he had reasonably expected intelligent co-operation or loving patience.

Let us, my dear brother, sustain him. This is my resolution. Depend upon it, a reality is in him which does not show itself all on the surface. There is a depth from which pure and living waters well up to refresh thirsty souls — supplied from the very source of life.

Yes, Abba understood. But patient as he was, the blow made Bronson ill and for weeks he was too weak to take up the burden of life again. But it was absolutely necessary that he support his family. As soon as he got to his feet again, he tried to get work at teaching in any school, in any place. But his attempts were vain. No school would have this iconoclast.

Emerson was his firm friend; indeed, he was the only person at that time in whom Bronson had confidence. The two men had a profound influence on each other. Emerson, reading Bronson's Journals, was lost in admiration of his friend and shows in his own essays how deeply he drew on Bronson's living waters. This excerpt from Bronson's diary, written at the moment life was utterly black for him, might easily have been the product of Emerson a decade later.

I have been (as is ever the habit of my mind) striving to apprehend the real in the seeming, to strip ideas of their adventitious phrases, and behold them in their order and power. I have sought to penetrate the showy terrestrial to find the heavenly things: I have tried to translate into ideas the language and images of spirit and thus to read God in his works. The outward I have seen as the visage and type of the inward.

Ever doth this same nature double its divine form and stand forth — now before the inner, now before the outer sense of man — at once substance and form, image and idea, so that God never shall slip wholly from the consciousness of the soul. Faith apprehends His agency even in the meanest and seemingly most trivial act, — wherever organ or matter undergo change of function or form, — Spirit king all in all.

Amidst all tumults and discomfortures, all errors and evils, Faith discerns the subtle bond that marries opposite natures, clinging to that which holds all in harmonious union. Faith unites opposites. It demolishes opposing forces. It melts all solid and opposite matters. It makes fluid the material universe. It hopes even in despair, believes in the midst of doubts, apprehends stability and order, even in confusion and anarchy and while all without is perturbed and wasting, it possesses itself in quietude and repose within.

Faith abides in the unswerving, is mighty in the omnipotent and enduring in the eternal. The soul, quickened by its agency, though borne on the wings of the mutable and beset by the winds of error and the storms of evil, shall ride securely under this directing hand to the real and the true.

In the midst of changes, it shall remain unchanged. For to such a faith is the divine order of God made known. All visible things are but manifestations of this order. Nature with all its change, is but the activity of this power. It flows round and obeys the invisible, self-anchored spirit. Mutability to such a vision is as the eddy that spirit maketh around its own self-circling agency, revealing alike in the smallest ripple and the mightiest surges the power that stirreth at the centre.

But this faith, which Bronson possessed to so extraordinary a degree, could feed the spirits of himself and his family, but not their bodies. And he had his moments of despair and hopelessness.

Apply to S——, school committee man, for the privilege of teaching the children of the primary school near Emerson's. But my services are declined. Are there no avenues open to the sympathies of my townspeople? O God, wilt Thou not permit me to be useful to my fellow men? Suffer me to use my gifts for my neighbor's children if not for themselves and thus bless the coming if not the present generation. How long, O Lord, how long wilt Thou try me by this exclusion from the active duties of the Church and the State? . . . Even the little primary school is denied me. But my own children still are within reach of my influence.

Light, O source of Light, give Thou unto Thy servant, sitting in the perplexities of this surrounding darkness! Hold Thou him steady to Thee, to truth and to himself : and in Thine own due time, give him clearly to the work for which Thou are thus slowly preparing him. . . .

For months it seemed as if no light would come. Emerson tried diligently to find work for Bronson but the net result is recorded below :

The plight of Mr. Alcott, the most refined and advanced soul we have had in New England, who makes all other souls appear slow and cheap and mechanical — a man of such courtesy and greatness that in conversation all others, even the intellectual, seem sharp and fighting for victory, and angry (he has the unalterable sweetness of a Muse) : yet because he cannot earn money by his pen or his talk, or by schoolkeeping, or bookkeeping, or editing, or any kind of manner, — nay, for this very cause, that he is ahead of his contemporaries, is higher than they and keeps himself out of the shop condescensions and smug art which they stoop to, — or unhappily need not stoop to, but find themselves as it were, born to, — therefore it is the unanimous opinion of New England judges that this man must die ! We do not adjudge him to hemlock or garroting. We are much too hypocritical and cowardly for that. But we not less surely doom him by refusing to protest against this doom or combining to save him and set him in employment fit for him and salutary for the

State — or to the Senate of fine souls which is the heart of the State.

Finally, Emerson urged him to give up school-teaching and take entirely to his pen.

Write! Let them hear or let forbear. The written word abides, until slowly and unexpectedly and in widely sundered places, it has created its own church. And my love and confidence in that silent Muse is such that, in circumstances in which I can easily conceive myself placed, I should prefer some manual or quite mechanical labor as a means of living, that should leave me a few sacred hours in the twenty-four, to any attempt to realize my idea in any existing forms called intellectual or spiritual : where, by defying every settled usage in society, I should be sure to sour my own temper.

Reading this suggestion, Bronson took stock of himself.

Ministers with few exceptions, regard me as an interloper in the theological fold and deem this (the school debacle) a fit occasion to make their sentiment known. They do not countenance my speculations nor look with friendly eye on my enterprise. Beside this, the teachers of the public schools in Boston, owing to the freedom of remark in which I indulge on the present state of education owe me no good will. Dr. Alcott, my cousin, has confidence in my intentions, approves my methods, generally, but distrusts the principles that guide me and looks with alarm on my supposed philosophy. In this he is not alone. Trinitarians know not what to make of me : Unitarians distrust me : unbelievers in Spirit cannot, of course, countenance me. Thus I am alone in the theological and philosophical world.

Thus, Bronson Alcott, aged forty, profound and felicitous thinker on education, found himself driven from the company of preachers and teachers.

CHAPTER XIV

Concord

EMERSON'S suggestions bore fruit. Abba and Bronson talked them over in the rooms in Boston, from which all the books and nearly all the furniture had disappeared and came to the momentous conclusion, that after all, though they could ruin Bronson in his profession, they could not take from him his trade. If he was not to be permitted to teach, he at least could do farm work. And so in April, 1840, the Alcotts removed from the Boston of their shattered dreams to Concord. Mrs. Alcott wrote her brother of the move.

We go to Concord for another experiment in the art of living in March. We have found a small cottage with a large garden and about an acre of ground, for $50 a year. It is about a mile from Mr. Emerson and a quarter of a mile from the village. . . . Mr. Alcott hopes to get his garden tools and to pay for the transportation from the sale of schoolroom furniture and from articles of household use which our little house will not accommodate. My ability to work is better than it has

213

been, but my constitution is more enfeebled than I am willing to realize. Yet the fact is forced upon me too often and powerfully not to carry conviction. But I will not anticipate evils. The quiet pure air and genial influences of the approaching season may promote a more vigorous state of health.

It was a brave thing and a wise one for Bronson to do — to return to the soil for a time; not only did he need the wholesome effect of work in the garden and fields, but Abba and the children were not in first class physical condition and the open skies, and meadows of Concord were tonic for them too. So Bronson worked for the neighboring farmers by day, tilled his own garden in the long spring and summer evenings and attended to the education of his Little Women. And for a time there was peace.

Bronson wrote to Samuel May, that spring:

I have planted myself again and am seeking to strike my roots into the soil, if it shall prove productive of even the scantiest sustenance of our common wants. My little garden and cottage lie low in the landscape: but there is the broad sky overhead and something still of its depth of azure in my hopes. If I have regrets, the chiefest is that in gaining Emerson for a neighbor, I have lost yourself. The river would flow by us more sweetly and the fields be greener were you also in our near neighborhood. . . . I wish we may find the new situation all we desire for earning an honest independence of others. And must I own that sometimes in our straitened moments, I have even wished some portion of the gifts with which I have been blessed had been withheld, if I might thereby have been brought into closer sympathy with the ordinary pursuits of mankind.

Oh, my brother! hardest of trials is this one, — of being sundered from my kind and left to tread the solitudes without an approving voice or kindly smile from anyone. Your sister is as brave and energetic as you could desire for meeting the new conditions; and we are doubly indebted and truly grateful for all the kind consideration of yourself and our friends.

Tilling the fields was always a labor of love to Bronson. He soon had a beautiful garden of his own and was making others, quite as fine, for neighboring farmers. Immediately, the physical condition of the whole family began to improve. Abba's splendid constitution was not really impaired and the color flushed back to her cheeks as it did to the children's. She could not so quickly return to her earlier enthusiasm for the simple life. It was one thing, she had found, to talk plain living and high thinking, and quite another thing to live it! Very slowly, she was permitting a schism to grow between her husband's philosophy and her own.

And yet, as much as is humanly possible, Bronson turned poverty into a beautiful and productive thing in his own and his children's lives. Although his days were given to the plow and the hoe, his profound mind was wrestling with intellectual problems, which the world at large was not to wrestle with for seventy-five years. He could not talk to the world, so he talked to his family, and in the intervals of heavy manual labor his girls heard conversations that gave them mental food fit for the gods.

He taught the children, daily. He wrote regularly. But, alas for Mr. Emerson's inspiring thought, no one would publish what Bronson wrote! Only the short-lived *Dial*, edited by Emerson, would print his essays and these were not remunerative and were laughed at by the *literati* of Boston. When that fact became conviction with Bronson he began to wonder what compromise he could make with life, he who never had compromised. Here he was a century ahead of his time : a beautiful vessel, laden with a spiritual and intellectual freight of incalculable importance to his fellow men. And because they were incapable of understanding the import of what he bore, his fellows refused to let him make port!

What was Bronson to do? He was too keen, intellectually, not to be aware fully of the importance of the contribution he had to make to America. He knew that of himself, as well as Emerson or Garrison or Thoreau knew it of him. Was he to give up any attempt to deliver his message to the world, and return, as he actually attempted at this time to do, to Seth Thomas' clock factory? To which was his responsibility the greater, to his family, or to that mysterious urge to give birth to his ideas at all costs, which is the peculiar earmark of genius?

Should he, he suggested to Abba, give up the intellectual life and return with Abba and the children to the farm at Spindle Hill? There, with all delivering their share of physical labor, the old farm could be made to produce physical comfort for all. But to wrest a living for a family from a Connecticut farm demanded so fearful a physical exertion that there was neither energy nor desire left for mental productivity. Was Bronson to take his family from Concord, from that charming intimacy with Emerson, Thoreau, Hawthorne, Elizabeth Peabody, all that group of supermen and women that New England had produced in this her greatest period? Emerson had a small private fortune which he had inherited. His essays would never have supported him. Hawthorne could sell his fiction and keep his family in comfort. Thoreau solved his problem by retiring to a hut in the woods and living the life of a hermit. Bronson Alcott, with an intellectual output greater than any of these men, had no private fortune, could not sell what he wrote, and having a wife and four children could not turn hermit.

It was Abba who had to make the decision. Poverty long since had ceased to have any horror for Bronson. It was Abba who was troubled by it. She worked no harder than Bronson, those early days in Concord, but in spite of the mental activity that never deteriorated, she had not the intellectual riches that made Bronson indifferent to outward circumstance. She had not his "repose." She was ambitious for the children, as Bronson was not.

Yet, brave generous and far-seeing, Abba made the decision rightly and at utter cost to herself. She could not go with him step by step in his phi-

losophy.   Yet she knew that it was a very great
philosophy and helped by her deep love for him,
she chose the harder lot.   They remained in Concord and although the world would have none of
him, Bronson kept on writing, worked now as a
farm laborer, now as a carpenter; a very great
Christian, carrying his heavy burden of thwarted
hopes in his own Pilgrim's Progress.

CHAPTER XV

The Molding of the Children

BRONSON loved the soil. I doubt if even Abba knew how sweet to him was that acre of land around the cottage. Abba was town-bred. But little Anna understood. Not but what Anna was a city product, but Anna was Bronson's daughter, flesh of his flesh.

And during all the years of their lives together, there was between Bronson and Anna an affinity of spirit that even the passionately loved wife or the deeply loved other daughters could not share.

One is conscious of this affinity as one reads Bronson's diaries. It was manifested all unconsciously on his part, from the time Anna was two years old and he began to contrast her with Louisa. It was, perhaps, not so much a difference in degree of love, as in kind.

Witness the letter, written by Bronson to Anna on her ninth birthday.

For Anna 1840

My dear Daughter:

With this morning's dawn opens a new year of
your life on Earth. Nine years ago you were sent,
a sweet babe, into this world, a joy and a hope to
your father and mother. After a while, through
many smiles and some few tears, you learned to
lisp the name of father and mother and to make
them feel how near and dear you were to their
hearts whenever you pronounced their names.
Now you are a still dearer object of love and hope
to them as your soul buds and blossoms under
their eyes. They watch the flower as it grows in
the garden of life and beside its sisters, scents the
air with its fragrance and delights the eye by its
colors. Soon they will look not only for fragrance
and beauty but for ripening and at last, ripe fruit
also. May it be the fruit of goodness; may its
leaves never wither: its flowers never fade: its
fragrance never cease: but may it flourish in per-
petual beauty and be transplanted in due time
into the Garden of God, whose plants are green
and bloom always: the amaranth of Heaven, the
pride and care of angels. Thus speaks your father
to you on this your birth-morn.

At the time of their removal from Boston, Anna
was nine years of age, Louisa eight and little Beth
was five. The children adored the cottage, set

low in a meadow not far from the river. It was quaint and comfortable, the same cottage that Louisa many years later was to describe as the Dovecot in "Little Women", when she established there Meg and her beloved John. As soon as the house was settled, Bronson began the children's school work. The family was up at dawn and before Bronson betook himself to the fields of the neighboring farm, the children had studied and recited with him for at least an hour. He gave them the same type of instruction that he had given the children in the Temple School. Even little Beth was required to print tiny letters to her grandmother and make an infantile entry in her diary.

After Bronson left for his farm work, Anna and Beth helped with the housework, while Louisa, the boy of the family, did the chores. They all were required to do a certain amount of sewing each day, a certain amount of weeding in the garden, and a certain amount of reading. It was a busy life but the three found plenty of time to play wild games in the fields and woods. They grew and throve so wonderfully that some of the bitterness of Boston began to slip from Abba's memory.

One Sunday in July, 1840, when Bronson came as usual at dawn to rouse the little girls, Anna looked up at him with her eyes of quick understanding and said, "Father, you look queer. You look tired and you look glad."

Bronson smiled, "I am both, my dear. It is very warm here in the house, and I am going into the garden. Mother is asleep. I wish you all to dress without waking her and come to me under the August sweeting tree. We will have our Sunday morning talk there."

There was some suggestion of mystery in his words that roused the three children to immense activity. Bronson had not been seated long on the bench beneath the August sweeting when Louisa, hair half-combed, pantalettes half unbuttoned at the knee, keen, dark little face vivid, came galloping along the path and hurled herself against him, with a hug and a kiss and a mischievous rumpling of his ash-blond hair. Anna, of course, had delayed to help the small Beth, but even these two dreamers were, for them, inordinately quick and shortly they appeared, hand in hand, Anna's gray eyes glowing under her orderly hair, and Beth's yellow ringlets bobbing sedately round her red cheeks.

There was a moment's scrabble when all three tried to sit on Bronson's knees at the same moment, but shortly this was settled by Louisa announcing that no boy ever sat in laps, and by Anna's saying, "I'm afraid I'll tire your knee, Father." So behold Bronson with apple-cheeked Elizabeth in his lap and a daughter on either side of him, obviously preparing to say something momentous. And the sunrise flooding river, meadows and orderly garden rows.

"Anna," said Bronson, with that indescribably inviting air of his, "what do we mean by a birth-day?"

"The day on which we are born," replied Anna promptly.

"What do you mean by being born, Louisa?" asked her father.

"Why, I mean coming into the world," replied Louisa briskly.

"But what comes into the world?" pursued Bronson.

"A person." Louisa spoke just before Anna's slow reply came. "The body and the mind of a child come on its birthday."

"Which is it that comes into the world first, a body or mind?" asked their father.

"Body," announced Louisa practically.

"Both," Anna was watching her father's face, with thoughtful eyes. "Birthday is the day on which the spirit is put into the body."

Little Beth suddenly wriggled. "It's the day the soul takes the body and brings it into the world."

Bronson caught his breath and looked down into the child's face. Beth's eyes were remote, seemingly fastened on the river. Louisa nodded. "That's the truth, Beth. The soul was living a long time before the body. I've always thought so."

Bronson paused a moment. A July robin was piping in the orchard and a bobwhite called from the meadow. "I will repeat you some lines," he said, "that were written by the poet who next to Coleridge understands children better than all other poets.

"Our birth is but a sleep and a forgetting,
    The soul that rises with us, our life's Star,
    Hath had elsewhere its setting,
    And cometh from afar:
    Not in entire forgetfulness,
    Not in utter nakedness,
    But trailing clouds of glory do we come
    From God, who is our home."

225

Bronson repeated the words slowly, his beautiful voice rising and falling clearly over the robin's notes. "What do the words mean, children?"

"I think I understand but I can't put it into words," said Louisa.

Anna did not speak. She only watched her father eagerly. Bronson turned to Beth. "Do you understand it, little dearest?" he asked.

"Well, you know," said Beth, her words dragging, "it *is* forgetting. Our life seems long to us. But it's a very short time to God."

She paused and Anna burst in quickly, "Yes, that's it! God tells the soul to go to earth and be born. And so that the soul won't be homesick for Him, he makes it forget all about where it came from."

"He puts it to sleep while it's being born," added Louisa. "That's a very kind thought for God to have. 'A sleep and a forgetting,'" she murmured. "That's beautiful."

"Yes! Beautiful!" agreed Bronson. "And now, tell me, Anna, what makes and shapes the body?"

"The soul," replied the oldest daughter.

"No! No!" cried Louisa. "The body is made and the soul just slips into it. Am I right, Father?"

"God," said Bronson carefully, "lets the earth build the body, just as he allows earth to build the trees and the birds. But earth builds the body for a special soul, always, under God's direction, so that when God sends that little bodiless soul down to earth, the body that has been making for it exactly fits it. And the little soul that He sends is always a portion of that same spirit from which he formed the father and the mother to whom he sends the little new-born soul. So that the lovely thing belongs not only to the God who sent it, but to the particular little body made for it, and also the father and mother of whose spirits it is a part."

He paused.

"That's why," exclaimed Anna, "we children are like both you and mother."

"That's why," agreed Bronson. "It's a lovely morning, is it not, children? No one could ask a lovelier day than this on which to be born, could one?"

"It's perfect," sighed Louisa. "I chose a horrid time to be born. November!"

"And so did I — March!" chimed in Anna. "I suppose there are children being born all the time, in all the months and all the days of the month."

"Yes," said Bronson, "that is why I wanted to talk to you about birthdays, this beautiful morning. For it is a birthday at our cottage, children."

"Whose?" demanded Louisa.

Anna clutched her father's arm.

"It's the birthday," said Bronson, his blue eyes deep and glowing, "of a little blue-eyed girl with a fuzz of yellow hair. Her name, your mother tells me, is Abba May Alcott. She arrived at the cottage fresh from heaven about an hour before I wakened you children, and your dear mother cuddled the baby thing up in her arms and they both went to sleep."

"I suppose it was a hard trip," volunteered Beth, her pink cheeks more deeply pink. "Can we keep her?"

"Did n't father say God sent them where they fitted?" cried Louisa. "I suppose we'll have to keep her! No matter how tired mother is."

Anna was standing before her father, her hand on his knee, looking deep into his eyes. "Of course we'll keep her," she murmured. "That's why you look so — so happy this morning, Father. And yet, somehow you look a little sad too, Father. Did you — would you rather she had been a little boy?"

STEPHENS COLLEGE
LIBRARY

MAY

"Oh, jinks, yes!" exclaimed Louisa, who was prancing up and down with excitement and pleasure. "Girls are getting to be an old story with us."

Neither Bronson nor Anna heeded her. "You know, Anna," her father was saying, "while we were in Boston, a little boy was sent to us, but somehow his little body was n't quite ready for him so he went away again. I hoped, and so did mother, that perhaps he 'd find courage to come back to us again. But that was not to be." Then as Anna's eyes flushed with sudden tears, he added gayly. "But since God decrees to us daughters of love instead of sons of delight, we 'll hopefully rear women for the new order of things. You 'll understand what that means before long, my dear."

He turned to Louisa who was listening silently, her dark eyes full of unfathomable thoughts, and smiled at her while he put Beth down from his knees.

"And now," he said, "let 's go and see if Abba May has really forgotten. Perhaps there 's something she can tell us." And he led the children back across the garden to the house. They entered quietly as though, since they had quit it, it had become a palace.

It was by lessons such as these that the Alcott children grew. Alcott's relation to the children was unique. He was more than teacher, more than father. But he in no way trespassed on Abba's prerogatives. Mrs. Alcott was a passionately affectionate and devoted mother and gave her whole life to the care of the four girls. And as she was an exceptional woman, intellectually, so did the children receive from her exceptional maternal training and care.

What Bronson gave to the girls belongs peculiarly to fatherhood and he gave of it without stint. Their mother taught them the small niceties of morals: the things any girl should know. Their father gave them the philosophy of morals, the broad base on which the fabric of Christianity rests. Their mother taught them practical charity. In all their poverty, as Mrs. Alcott wrote her brother, "I never have allowed the children to neglect those more destitute than themselves." Bronson heartily endorsed this, but he went further. While his wife, poor soul, was never reconciled to the hard conditions of their living, he made of their poverty a thing chaste, noble and serene, and taught his children that their poverty was an honorable thing, a condition that,

rightly looked upon, would give them the distinc-
tion of soul nothing else could give.

There are many of the finest aspects of life that a
man can teach his children with authority, because
of the position in the world his sex gives him;
aspects that a woman can teach only from hearsay
and with consequent lack of force. Not one
father in ten thousand takes advantage of his own
peculiar prestige in these things, or realizes that
there are phases of sex, of religion, of conduct, that
only a father can give. Thrice fortunate the child
whose father will take advantage of the privilege
Nature has given him!

None of the Alcott girls responded to Bronson's
teachings as did Anna. Not one of them but was
profoundly influenced by them, but none of the
children suffered as did Anna over the solitude
that was forced on her father those first years in
Concord. She had not Louisa's fighting nature —
a nature that Louisa inherited from both sides of
the house, the persistence from her father, the
aggressiveness from her mother. She was gentle
and sensitive with the true artist's susceptibility of
temperament. A very great actress probably
was spoiled by Anna's lack of fighting blood. She
had not the long unbreakable determination of

the little boy on Spindle Hill who left the oxen in the furrow while he impersonated Christian on his many adventures. But she was a very lovely human being whose belief in goodness and beauty heartened her father through many a bitter hour.

Her diary was kept almost from babyhood with the meticulous care characteristic of all she did. Observe the diction of this nine-year old child.

Boston, February 12, 1840. Here is a sentence which I analyzed this morning. It is from a letter which I wrote to mother from Wolcott (Conn.) when I was five years of age. I was with father on a visit to Grandmother. I copy the letter :

"My dear Mother,
I have to go away by myself and cry because I want to see you so much and little sister Lisy and Louisa. Dr. Fuller is coming to cure Grandmother. i shall see you in a few days. You have a splendid husband."

Anna

(Analysis)

Things	Activities	Sorts	Relations
Mother	go	dear	to
Lizzy	cry	away	-by
Louisa	want	so	and
	see	much	

Concord, Sept. 1, 1840. I helped mother iron and tend baby beside having my lessons with father. My sums were all right today. I read several pieces of poetry to father from the Commonplace Book of poetry. Father read us the Fairy Tale of Order and Disorder. I had a very interesting talk with Father about Jesus. He explained to me several things I wanted to know about what he did: about his feeding the five thousand people and about raising the dead to life, and stilling the tempest. I like conversations with father.

Thursday, Sept. 3, 1840. Father read from Pilgrims' Progress about the pictures at the Interpreter's house and made some pictures of our appetites and passions. We had baby in the school, and she seemed almost to talk. She said, "coo, coo." She is not quite six weeks old. Elizabeth said and wrote almost all of her letters and Louisa wrote some with her pen. I was interested most in the conversation on God and the soul. I can see how a great many things can be without my seeing, tasting, hearing, smelling, touching or feeling them.

Sunday, Nov. 4, 1840. Louisa and I went to meeting and father too. We sat in Mr. Emerson's seat. When we were coming home it was raining and Mr. Thoreau asked us to go in and wait till it had done raining so we went in and took dinner there.

Monday, Nov. 13, 1840. Father and mother were putting down carpets today and father did n't hear our lessons, but Louisa. I did not feel as happy as I would have felt if I had been more useful. Mother was very busy today.

Thursday, Dec. 10th, 1840. I and Louisa did n't spell our lesson well, so father let us go without any dinner. I sewed with mother in the afternoon and played in the evening. I went out and shoveled snow before I sewed.

Wednesday, Dec. 16, 1840. Father read and talked to us about curing our bad habits. I made a resolution and hope I shall keep it. He said that till we could be gentle and kind to each other we could not have the pleasure of tending baby. I had rather have most any punishment than that. In the afternoon mother went to the village and Louisa and I sewed while she was gone. It was very pleasant in the morning but it was dark in the afternoon and hailed a little and in the evening it snowed. It came down so gently that we did not hear it and when we woke up the next morning the ground was covered with snow but there was some beautiful clouds they were red and golden.

Tuesday, Dec. 23, 1840. I helped mother with baby some. I did not have lessons today. The time that I could have had them I used in dressing my doll. I do not think I did right then. Father got breakfast this morning all himself. after breakfast I tended baby. she is not well she is a sweet little thing and I love her very much. We read about Jesus walking on the water and Peter sinking in it. I like to read about Jesus, because he is so good. Father is the best man in the world, now.

Tuesday, Dec. 29, 1840. Christmas I found some goodies in my stocking. In the evening cousin Hamilton brought some books for us children. There was Northcote's Fables, Sowing and Reaping, Book of Rhymes, Among the Birds, Scripture History, Alphabet of Natural History and Mother Goose's Melodies . . . Yesterday Louisa and I wrote a letter to the Russells. I copy a letter which mother wrote me on Christmas. Here it is:

"Dear Anna. I wish I could put into your heart the real bon bons as easily as I can place in your stocking these artificial ones. Your Christmas will be a happy one just as far as you make it a good one. The presence of your little baby sister will make it merry if you give her your gentle arms for her carriage, your soft bosom for her pillow, and your soft voice for her music. She was not with us last Christmas. Let us be happier for her sake than we ever were before. Let us be patient because she is tender. Let us be gentle because she is an angel and may put out her little wings and flutter back to God who only gave her to us to make us happy on earth. Love your sister Louisa and be patient, love Elizabeth and be gentle. Love Abby and be kind. Love Father and be obedient. Love Mother and be dutiful. Love your duty and you will be happy.

Mother
Christmas Eve."

To Anna from her father while she was on a visit to Boston:

Concord, Thursday Eve, 14 May, 1841.

My daughter,

How seems the great city to you, with its nice men and women, its pale, prim children, its dulness and confinement? And how now, the little cottage under the hill, with its spaces for racing, loud speaking, and all the freedom to do as you want to whensoever you step on its threshold? Homesick, are you! Well, 't will do you some good — 't will show you the difference between places and people, between being homesick and sick of home and bring you back with your love all new. I miss you! but the baby misses you more, though Louisa's ready arms support her long within doors and out: in garden and street: to barn and bridge: but still the little Sweet wants you again, I know. Today I planted some peas and other garden vegetables — the sun showing his face to us after veiling it so long. In a few days the earth will tell her joy and thankfulness by growing tokens; as we do now all, by grateful looks and gentler words, sunshine within as sunshine without.

Louisa plies her hand nimbly with her mother or flies like a bird over the garden and fields : mother's economies all prosper well : and that silent man with a pen complains no more of noise ! Concord it now is ! Two make peace. Three bring discord. . . . Be gentle and docile : (look that word out in your dictionary) while with your friends : simple and frank in your words and behavior. Suffer no one to tempt you by entreaty from your feeling of Duty : Say, Yes, or No, not to please others but your own conscience : and when you return to your home, your eye and manner will tell the Story of your Fidelity to us all.

Thus writes,
Your Father.

Write us soon.
For Anna Bronson Alcott

CHAPTER XVI

The Last Experiment

FOR two years Bronson labored without light for the future. He swung the scythe in the summer, and in the winter he chopped wood and managed to earn thereby enough to keep his family out of want. It was, as he wrote his brother Junius, an almost hopeless period. But he heard cheering news in the spring of 1842. Some one had established in England a school, based on Bronson's theories and had named it Alcott House. Emerson, enormously proud of his friend, began to urge him to visit England, talk to Carlyle, see the school and receive there if possible the recognition America denied him. As for funds, Emerson offered to raise them.

Abba was enthusiastically for the venture. Junius Alcott agreed to spend the summer at the cottage, taking Bronson's place as wage earner, and in May, hardly daring to believe in the wonder of it, Bronson found himself on board a sailing vessel with ten sovereigns in his pocket and a bill of exchange for twenty pounds.

He remained in England all summer, returning to Concord in October. He got on well with the English Transcendentalists and wrote charming letters home to Emerson, to Thoreau, to Samuel May, to Abba. But the most quaintly delightful are the two or three he sent to his children.

For Louisa May Alcott,
    Elizabeth Sewall Alcott
         and
    Abba May Alcott
        Concordia Cottage — from their father,
          15 July, 1842.

My dear Girls :

I think of you all every day and desire to see you all again : Anna with her beauty-loving eyes and sweet visions of graceful motions, of golden hues and all fair and mystic shows and shapes — Louisa with her quick and ready services, her agile limbs and boundless curiosity, her penetrating mind and tear-shedding heart, alive to all moving, breathing things — Elizabeth with her quiet-loving disposition and serene thoughts, her happy gentleness, deep sentiment, self-centered in the depths of her affections — and last, but yet dearest too in her joys and impetuous griefs, the little Abba with her fast falling footsteps, her sagacious eye

239

and auburn locks . . . and mother too, whose unsleeping love ·and painstaking hands provide for your comforts and pleasant things and is your hope and stay and now more near and important to you while I am taken from your eyes. All and each of you I have in my mind : daily I see you in my thoughts and as I lay my head on my pillow at night or wake from sleep in the morning . . . nor can the tumbling waters hide my group of loves from my eyes : the little cottage there behind the Elm, the garden round, strawberry red or colored vines . . . or corn barn play house, or street or bridge or winding stream, or Anna or Louisa, their lessons loved (and learned by heart, not rote) and Lizzy too with little Ab in parlor, study, chamber, lawn, with needle, book or pen . . . and so you see, my gentle girls, I cannot leave you quite : though my body is far away my mind is near and all the while, I hear and see and touch and think and feel your very selves — the life that lives in all you are and say and do, the mind, the Heart, the Soul — the God that dwells in you. And now be loving little girls and grow more fair with every day and when I come to see my garden plot then shall my flowers scent the fields and I shall joy in every scent they lend, in every tint and form they wear. So now, my dears, adieu.

Let mother read this with you and talk long and sweetly with her about what is in it and then kiss her all and each other and then her all again for Father's sake.

Bronson brought back with him from England a new enthusiasm. But, more than that, he brought the enthusiasm in the embodied form of one Charles Lane and his son, William. Lane was an English philosopher who had conceived an enormous admiration for Bronson. He wanted Bronson to join him in establishing a community for the carrying out of their ideals of living. He had sufficient money to buy a farm. To this farm he proposed to call other kindred spirits where they could delve, reap and spin, feeding and clothing themselves by their own hands, free of all the complicated financial system of the world.

The Lanes settled down in the Alcotts' cottage for the winter and the new philosopher became the central point of interest for Emerson, Thoreau, Hawthorne, Miss Fuller, and the project was discussed from every possible angle. Abba found the winter particularly trying. The cottage was a difficult place with five children and all the philosophers, although never were the girls better taught than during these months when Lane, who was a musician, took great pains with their piano lessons and their mathematics, while Bronson labored assiduously with their other branches of learning, what time he was not chopping wood to pay the grocery bills. Two of his characteristic letters to Anna at this time have survived.

Dearest Anna:

Shall I tell you how much pleasure you give me by your well meant and by no means ineffectual endeavors to improve yourself and to aid in improving your sisters in goodness and knowledge, your kindness and gentleness sometimes, your patience and care at other times, the thoughtful love that leads you to help your father and mother in the care of the household and of the little inmates of our cottage during this winter season when we all are brought near to each other and have to do many things near which we could do better if separate and with more room and ampler means of doing them. Our cot is small and our best and only way is to make small our wants, to have few and these so simple that they all can be supplied without pain or cost to anyone. You are growing fast into a woman, and you can do more for your sisters' good than even your father and mother because you are more with them, — and they will become what you are in a great many ways that you hardly can believe now. Go on, my daughter in your good resolutions, your kind manners and give me yet deeper content by your conduct. We

are all now striving to do all we can for each other :
we shall all be helped by the Good and all provident
Helper and if we deserve better things they will be
given us. . . . The cottage never seemed to me
in a more lively and improving state than just now.

Your Father.

Cottage, 3rd Feby 1843
   For Anna

Concord, 16 April 1843

My daughter :
   Your pretty present of a place mark for my
Books gave me the pleasure which every affectionate act of yours always yields me.   It is a fit token
of your regard for a father's tastes and an apt symbol of a daughter's interest in like pursuits.   It is
neatly wrought and delicately imagined and as
delicately conveyed to me.   Be assured that I
shall prize it and that it will serve to remind me in
my readings not only of a daughter's kindred tastes
but of her skilfulness in handling the needle. . . .
   My daughter, upon you it devolves to sustain
the hopes and interests your father has so long
espoused and amidst many hindrances endeavored to carry into eternal life . . . .   A career of
noblest usefulness awaits you.   You are favored
above many of the daughters of men. . . .   Orna-
ment your mind and heart with pure manners,
cherish every divine trait in your being, and be all
that the love and confidence of a Father can desire

or portray. Dear Anna, I am yours in the depth of a serene and confiding affection which more by silence than speech, through acts rather than by words, would manifest its constant and abiding presence.

Father.

Bronson was absolutely enchanted with Lane's idea. Here was the solution for his terrible economic problem. Here was protection for his family. Here was material for his theories. Abba was skeptical at first but when she observed Bronson's attitude, she consented to follow him. She never had seen him so enthusiastic. Even the Temple School in Boston in its early days had not encouraged him to the same degree. Bronson in this mood was not to be influenced. When Emerson showed interest and hope in the scheme, Abba packed up her household furnishings and her children, and in the spring of 1843 went with Bronson to the one hundred-acre farm, Fruitlands, near the tiny village of Harvard. Perhaps, she thought, it might solve the never-ending problem of living.

It was seven months before the experiment dwindled into nothingness. Looking back at it through the perspective of more than three quarters of a century, one sees it as something heroic and pathetic; this honest attempt of two idealists to live up to their ideals. Who that has sweated with the problem of how to earn bread for one's loved ones and not thereby lose all the fine aspects of life, can think of that futile experiment without respect!

It failed, of course, in spite of the fact that Bronson nearly killed himself at farm work, with Lane not far behind him in strenuousness, and that Abba, the only woman in the scheme, for the greater part of the period, did the work of three people. Lane and Bronson Alcott could not agree on the practical essentials of the scheme. The scanty harvest had been gathered before Bronson could admit to himself that there was a chance of failure. What finally got under his skin was the realization that Lane wished to break up his family life. The Englishman did not believe in families. He told Bronson that the great handicap to his success was Abba and the little girls.

Abba watched Lane at first with contemptuous amusement and then as she saw the intellectual influence he gained over her husband she was filled with consternation. Fruitlands suddenly became a horror to her, a place of lurking demons waiting to destroy her family. She turned against Lane with all the fire and venom of her passionate nature.

As the fall days marched toward bitter winter, Bronson grew more and more silent. He was perfectly well aware of the struggle Charles Lane and Abba were having over him, but it was a struggle in a mist; a struggle, the details of which were not worth piercing the fog to observe. For Bronson was waging a fight with himself, a fight in which, he told himself, something within him must die.

He acknowledged that Abba was not fitted for the sort of life that was entirely congenial to him. He, himself, would have been satisfied as Thoreau was, with a hermit's hut and with bread, honey, fruit and vegetables which he could produce himself for his sustenance. In theory Abba agreed with him and she believed herself to be a person of simplest wants and ambitions. But as a matter of fact she was wholly feminine. She wanted to live as her neighbors lived, her girls to have the things that other girls had. With all her might and main she upheld Bronson in his philosophy of life. But she could not reconcile herself to allowing him to apply that philosophy to herself and the girls! And Bronson, loving her with all the single-

have it call conditionally. Remember dear, to pick up your things. Don't depend on anyone to do this for you.

Mother.

But "Father" did not go over to get the baggage. In the fortnight that elapsed before Anna's return, Bronson gave up the struggle and turned to the third alternative.

On the moonlit November night of Anna's return, it was tomboy Louisa who met her at the stage, and not her father.

"Papa is sick," announced Louisa, seizing Anna's valise in stout boy fashion. "They 've all gone, the fat, the lean, the lazy and the learned. I 'm awful glad." Louisa at eleven had very few illusions about human beings.

The two young girls started across the moonlit fields, Louisa taller than Anna, striding out at a mighty pace. "But Lu, dear," panted Anna, "what 's the matter with father? Is he very sick?"

"Well, he just lies there and says nothing and eats nothing. I think he 's tired out and disappointed. You know as well as I do that he did about three times his share of the farm work, all summer and fall. Poor mother is nearly distracted over him."

Anna began to sob softly. Louisa dropped back to put her arm round her sister's shoulder. "Don't cry, Nan! You've got me! Just lean on me. And don't let's stop here to cry," looking around at the stubble field in which they were standing, "I must finish the chores. That horrible cow's got to be milked and the wood got in for the night."

"I can't cry after I get home. You'll have to let me have it out here," Anna scrubbed her face vigorously with her handkerchief, while Louisa patted her shoulder and nodded. After a moment, Anna picked up her bundles and trudged on after her sister.

The girls entered the house via the kitchen. Mrs. Alcott was making spearmint tea at the stove. She turned, her face vivid with welcome, a tall, magnificently proportioned woman with Louisa's own fine, flashing dark eyes.

She kissed Anna half a dozen times, seeming not to note the traces of tears on her oldest daughter's cheeks. Anna threw off her wraps and warmed her hands at the fire. She looked older than her twelve years, in spite of the mass of chestnut curls in her neck and the childish curve of her round, red cheek.

STEPHENS COLLEGE
LIBRARY

"Let me take the spearmint in to father," she said.

Mrs. Alcott nodded. "Perhaps he'll take it from you: he's eaten nothing for days. He has deliberately willed himself to die," she added, her lips quivering.

Anna took the little tray and made her way to her father's room.

Bronson lay on the wide bed, a long figure with classic profile in the flickering candlelight. Anna set the tray on the stove and crossing to the bed, lifted her father's hand to her lips.

"Father! Aren't you glad to see me? You wrote me to come home, you know."

Bronson opened his eyes. "Darling Anna!" he said huskily.

"I've brought you some hot tea. You'll take it, Father, for my sake."

Her father slowly shook his head. "I've no need of it, dear. I'm going on a long journey and I'm going alone."

"No!" exclaimed Anna. "Think, Father, of your work!"

"It has been too early for my work," Bronson spoke in a husky, half-broken voice. "I am a hindrance to mother and you girls, . . . the solitude is too great for me."

"You wrote me last spring," Anna spoke rapidly, "that I was to carry on your hopes and interests. I'm still only a little girl. You have no right to leave me until you have taught me what your hopes and interests are. I think God will think if you teach one child thoroughly all your ideas, that that's a great deal better than lying down to die because selfish people like those we've been living with here at Fruitlands won't heed you."

Bronson, who had closed his eyes, opened them to gaze with great and tender affection on Anna's pleading face.

"All that I have gleaned in a lifetime, I can tell you in a few moments," he said. "You are to go on with my studying and teaching of children. . . . I have studied them because by so doing, I was studying Spirit in the purest form that it presents itself to the observation of men. When I study the spirit of a child, I am in a charmed world, the very heart of the Ideal beats before me. Divinity unveils itself here. This study fits me to understand the inner life of humanity. It teaches me to understand not only nature but God. Whoso would be a prophet, let him contemplate the spirit of childhood for here are all the causes that effectuate the changes of the future — Yes, every child is a prophet sent from God." . . .

Bronson paused, unseeing eyes on the flickering candle. Anna, startled and pale, kissed his cheek. "Father! Dear, dear Father," she whispered; "come back!"

"The years have passed," said Bronson, unheeding, "and Time has unveiled the secrets of things to my vision and not till I find the solution that satisfies the Spirit, will I rest. In the resplendent mirror of childhood I have tried to read the Eternal word, that I might interpret it to others, but most of all to the child himself, to save him from the loss of his innocence. Fain would I stand beside him at his entrance into the flesh, accompany him in his transit across space and open out to him while he lives in Time, the reassurance of God within him, the You before it returns to the bosom of the Father."

Again, as the weary voice paused, Anna stooped and kissed him. "Father! O my dear Father, do not leave me! Stay to teach me what you mean by all those things."

"You will not forget them," said Bronson, focusing his tired blue eyes on the young girl's face. "And when you are older, you will carry on my researches. You, too, will be too early for the world to understand. And you will find the solitude, as I have, intolerable."

"No!" cried Anna. "I cannot let you go! Or if you must go, take me with you away from all the hard work and the poverty."

As if her last words had been a blow, Bronson started and drew his work-stained hand across his forehead. Then he clasped Anna's fingers within his own and said, "My darling girl, if only I could teach you that you make your own poverty by your desires. It is your craving for physical things that makes you poor . . . as for work — nothing brings the essential content to human beings that does toil with the hands to bring fields to fruition. Anna! Anna! Cannot I give you some of my own simple content?"

"Yes," whispered Anna. "If you will stay and let me watch you and do as you do. Oh, I know, I know! though I am so young, how lonely you have been. But let your love balance that. Even though mother disagrees with you, think how she loves you. And I — Father, I cannot live without you. Stay with me, Father, in that journey across space, you speak of. How can you bear not to practice what you preach?"

There was something unbearably poignant in the way that the gigantic dreamer looked with inexpressible yearning into the young girl's face. "Anna, can I be useful if I stay?"

And there was all the conviction of the prophet in Anna's reply. "You have your greatest work yet to do. You've just been getting ready for it."

A silence fell between them, broken by the crackle of maple logs in the Franklin stove and the soft sound of voices from the kitchen. Bronson stared at this child of his greatest love, beads of sweat breaking out on lip and forehead, as a struggle of intellect and soul whose magnitude none might know took place within him. At last, with the vague and charming twist of humor on his lips that was so dearly familiar to Anna, he glanced toward the spearmint tea, simmering on the stove.

"If that is one of mother's concoctions, I will drink it."

With shaking fingers, Anna held the cup to his lips and Bronson drank deeply of the fragrant beverage. As he finished there was a soft, quick step at the threshold and Abba entered the room. She glanced at the empty cup. Bronson smiled

255

at her and held out his arms, and as her mother with a little sob crossed to be folded in that loved embrace, Anna tiptoed to the kitchen where Louisa was waiting with her belated supper.

CHAPTER XVII

His Children

AND so the Alcotts returned to Concord and Bronson again sought to place himself in some sort of harmonious relation with the economic scheme of life as it is. Two fragments of his writings at this time give as clear a picture of his state of mind as the longer entries in his diaries. The first is extraordinarily modern in form.

As from himself he fled,
   Outcast, insane,
Tormenting demons drove him from the gate.
   Away he sped
Casting his woes behind,
   His joys to find,
   His better mind.

   Recovered
   Himself again,
Over his threshold led,
   Peace fills his breast.
   He finds his rest :
Expecting angels his arrival wait.

257

The other, a letter to his daughters, give his answer to Lane's ideas about family.

For all — 1843, from Father.

My children: I will show you what is beautiful, beautiful indeed, — surpassing all other things in beauty and more to be desired than everything upon which the eye can rest . . . that for which the world and all its glories were made, for which life itself was given . . . for which man, woman and child were furnished and sent with the body — that which is the happiest work of the Holiest Father's mind and Hands, — it is a pure and happy, a kind and loving family, a home where peace and joy and gentle quiet abide, always . . . around whose hearth gather serene and loveful countenances, where every hand is quick to help, every foot swift to save, every eye agile to catch the wishes and every ear the wants of others: where every day is a long and well-gotten lesson of love and wisdom and patient resignation and steady trust in that Good and Generous Power that sends Health and Hope and Peace.

The Heavens above and the earth beneath can cover nor support no more comely building than such a Home.   'T is a holy spot, a temple wherewith God himself enters and therein abides with his angels.   Your Father.

To the Young Inmates of the Cottage while supping around the hearth.

The Fruitlands experiment turned the eyes of New England again toward Bronson and there was an enormous amount of derision and laughter. And yet, there were some who came to scoff who remained to pray. Folk who came from Boston to talk with Emerson frequently found Bronson Alcott in that hospitable library and listened to him talk. That golden tongue which had enthralled the children of the Temple School could not fail to touch them, though his pen had left them cold. Young James Russell Lowell, whose wit had often slashed Bronson to the quick, was one of those who visited Concord at this time. He went back to Boston to write a poem about Bronson:

> Hear him but speak and you will feel
> The shadows of the portico
> Over your tranquil spirit steal,
> To modulate all joy and woe
> To one subdued, subduing glow;
> Above our squabbling business hours,
> Like Phidean Jove, his beauty lowers,
> His nature satirizes ours;
> A form and front of Attic grace,
> He shames the higgling market place,
> And dwarfs our more mechanic powers —

With Emerson's unremitting support, with Thoreau and Hawthorne adding their written and spoken admiration, timid souls in Boston took courage and began to ask Bronson to come in to town to give lectures on his beliefs.   People would not read what he wrote, nor permit him to teach their children, but they would pay him to talk to themselves.   These lectures, with the carpentering and wood cutting, made it possible for the Alcotts to live.   They even in 1845 bought a house that had been used by a man who raised pigs in his front yard, and Bronson set to work to make it a thing of beauty.

He was forty-six now and his experiments in remaking the theories of the world were ended. From now on, with as many years before him as had passed behind him, he must be content with whatever vague results might be won from the lectures and from the records in a diary that no one would read, let alone publish.

Thrown thus back on himself, he became more and more absorbed in the education of his children. Except for one short experience in a Concord school, none of the girls received any teaching save what he gave them.

Her conversation with her father on that moon-

lit November night had a permanent effect on
Anna. From that moment she was determined
to be a teacher, such a teacher as her father would
wish her to be. Louisa was fearfully bored with
the idea of teaching. She, at eleven, after giving
the Fruitlands experiment the benefit of the scru-
tiny of her exceedingly canny young eye, decided
that never would she choose a profession which
could visit such suffering on those who chose it as
did teaching. She, herself, was going to be an
actress, — although as a matter of fact she had
not Anna's really extraordinary dramatic ability.
And with the return to Concord she began writing
and acting plays that still are preserved. They
are quaint, stilted and melodramatic, copied into
notebooks by Anna's exquisite pen. Her intense
interest in the stage and in writing for it, as well
as Anna's love of teaching and acting, were the
direct results of Bronson's methods of teaching,
beginning with those charming winter twilights
in Boston when the baby sisters danced and inter-
preted fables in the fire's glow.

Little Abba May responded more than the others
to the picture-making suggestions and even at
five or six was drawing with a keen feeling for line
and perspective.

Elizabeth, at ten, was very musical, would, in fact, have given all her little days to the piano had her father not insisted on other things. Her Journal shows how well those other things were absorbed.

Concord, April 27, 1845: It was a sunny morning. I carried my dollies on the hill, then went to the village. I sat in a cherry tree and wrote my Journal. I read to Abba about Oliver Twist and she cried because he was so poor.

May 1st, Father took us to Mr. Emerson's in Mr. Watt's hay cart. We danced around the May pole, and I had a very pleasant time. Mr. Emerson said he would take us to ride in the woods. But it rained so we came back home. After the shower Abba and I played in the barn. We made dirt cakes and a little wagon to draw our dollies in.

May 2 . . . I made my bed and read in Fireside stories until school time. I wrote in my Journal and did two sums with two figures. Anna helped me before Father came into the schoolroom. He asked me to write the order for the day's doings and I put it down on the next page.

A Day's Order

Rise at half past five   dress and bathe   Breakfast at half past six   Sing and make my bed   Play till ten Study in the schoolroom till twelve Dinner Wash the dishes and sweep the kitchen Play till three Sew till five Supper Read or play with Abba — I write my journal first when I come in to school.

Father took us in the woods with him to get some trees. The dog went with us. It was very pleasant. While Father was digging the pretty Larch and Spruce trees, I picked some handsome green mosses for my attic chamber. Father gave me some little pines and larches to put in my garden. Father and I walked up the hill coming home to lighten the load for the horse. After dinner, I washed the dishes. We thought of going to Waldron Water for some hemlocks, but did not. I read in "Undine" a while, then went to the brook and got white violets and snow drops.

Tuesday, May 4. After lessons I sat in my chamber and read "Undine." Mr. Emerson took us to ride. We went to the place where he is going to build a Lodge to study in. He drove us to Waldron Pond and took Gary Pratt, Ellen Emerson and me in a boat. It was very pleasant on the water — At breakfast father read about Jesus riding the colt in Jerusalem.

Monday, August 3, 1846. I picked some beans to give Mr. Bull and washed the napkins and towels. After dinner I ironed and made a little bonnet for my doll. Abba and I played cards and checkers.

Monday, Sept. 28. I sorted some apples in the cellar. Anna kept school for us. I wrote my Journal and studied a Geography lesson in Peter Parley's Geography about South America. It is a very large country and Gold and Silver are brought from it. They are dug from the earth and diamonds are washed from the mountains. At recess, Louisa wheeled us in the wheelbarrow down the hall. When we came in I drew two pitchers. I had a very pleasant morning. Louisa and I picked some beans and shelled them for dinner. I picked over some potatoes and learnt a Geography lesson about Europe and drew a pitcher from the drawing book.

Sunday, Oct. 28. We went to Mr. Emerson's. Father read us a hymn and a Story. After I came home I learned a piece of poetry called "My Mother's Sigh", and read some more Hoary Head. It was a very pleasant day. I sat on the hill and read a good while. I played with Abba and we set a table for our dollies and dressed them to play go to meeting. Louisa and I ran in the garden and played sell "vegetables and fruit."

Thursday — Nov. 1. I cleaned the knives and swept the sitting room and washed the hearth. I swung Abba and we painted some pictures. I read her a story of the "Suspected Boy" which she liked very much. Then we played in mother's chamber. We played with Louisa and Anna, "Travel."

And so goes the innocent chronicle through its far too few pages : the story of a happy child.

The happiness was to persist through her short life, for Beth was the very darling of the household. Her father could not speak or write to her without a display of tenderness that after all these years brings moisture to one's eyes.

June 24, 1844.

My very dear Elizabeth :

I have always given you some little presents of gifts and notes on your Birthdays. Last year, we celebrated this day, you remember with pleasure, I daresay, at Fruitlands. Then I wrote a little Ode for you, and all of us were very happy in the grove and gave you our little gifts. Today we celebrate in a different way. I have no roses now for you : but this little note, with a pretty China Cameo of "Love." The cameo will be a handsome toy to have a place among your nicely arranged treasures and remind you of your father's pleasure in your quiet, neat and orderly ways and help to make you more so as you grow older and other toys of furniture and care of house-wifery and of living things are entrusted to you.

Sweet hopes your Father has of you, my quiet and thoughtful Child. Surely nothing on your part shall disappoint him. I hope you will enjoy the company of your friends on this Birthday. Kind mother has done much to make the time pleasant to you and your sisters have been very busy to minister to you. And now as I write, dear Anna brings me a useful gift to present you, lest I should chance to be unfurnished, or forget to do as all your friends delight in doing. So I present it with my other gift, the Beautiful and the Useful, together.

From your hopeful
Father

Hillside, Concord
24 June, 1845

My very dear Elizabeth :

Your dear little head is so full of loving and quiet stillness that I will not disturb its calm thoughtfulness by any words of grave wisdom. And so let me furnish your Feet with a neat covering in which your footsteps may be as light as your gentle Heart and swift as your Obedience. So take these from your Father, on this your tenth Birthday.

Father

P. S.   I hope the Shoes will fit your ready Feet as nicely as does your still little Head the shape of your Mind.

Concord, Hillside, Friday, 3 P.M.
December 10, 1847

Dear Anna : Elizabeth has just left us to pass some time with Miss Robie in Boston. Your Mother, Louisa and Abby have just returned from the Station with tearful eyes and a sadness at the heart. And little Abby declares there is no pleasure for her now in this old ugly house. The house is, indeed, shorn of some of its attractiveness now that the pure little maid is gone whose gentle assiduities to all its inmates were so uninterrupted and so sweet. But she will reap advantage from the change and we shall learn the more of her worth. The Good God will protect so much goodness, wherever it may abide : nor can she fail to find sources of happiness in any employment that may be given her. Families must swarm sometimes, and it is well for her and yourself too, perhaps, to seek fields of richer Thyme than grow about the old Hive, and fall to honey-making for yourselves. Since all true and lasting enjoyment must be sipped from the cup of our exertions alone. I well remember the time of leaving my own home at the age of twelve and the strength which a few months' absence gave to my youthful character. So it will be with yourself and with Elizabeth, I doubt not. No Home was ever quite sufficient for the mind of a Child, and but few for the Heart and Hand.

But yet, knowing this as I do and feeling the truth of it every day more and more, I am not reconciled to that necessity which sends two of our daughters from our threshold — "God be with ye," a truth I have never questioned as regards my absent daughter.

Your Father.

To Elizabeth at Mr. Sewall's in Boston.
Hillside, Concord,
Sunday Afternoon, Sept. 5, 1848

He wrote at the same time to Elizabeth who was visiting in Boston.

Dear Elizabeth:

I am unwilling this letter pacquet should go forth from us without my own little note to you, along with mother's and sister's big and bigger letters. I was pleased to see you leave home which you love so much so cheerfully and though I miss you every meal and especially every breakfasting, I am quite willing to have you look at the great town, and townsfolk and find how you like them, with your own dear eyes and for yourself. You never have left home without taking the best of it along with you. Some one or more of us has always accompanied you, and I shall not be surprised to learn of your not finding the new enjoyments dear to you, even with your kind friends in town. But Homesickness, if it come to you, is easily cured, home is so near and you are free to invite the swift steamsteed to bear you to our threshold. I left home to spend a month when I was about your age and so long a month was there never before nor since has been and my courage failed me and I was glad to return to the familiar places and delights at the weeks' end unshamed. But you have more courage and more love perhaps withal than I had and so will brave out your week or more with your accustomed fortitude, hiding your feelins in silence. . . . But come or stay we shall all love you and such as you, forever, dear Elizabeth.

Today you have been to church, I fancy. How did it seem? the spacious Church, the courtly people, the gowned Priest, the service of prayer and praise, the pealing anthem and the pealing bells? Beautiful, most beautiful where sincere devotion lends and homage to the All Beautiful prompts! Write to us about it for I hear that you will write to us tomorrow.

Little Abby has written out her lonesomeness in her little note to you and will count the days of your absence till it is ended. We all have had a quiet day. This morning I gathered the apples and saved some fine golden Porters for you which we send along with other tokens of our regard. Your kind friends will share these with you. And I will persuade myself that when you leave them to come to us you will leave much love and regard behind you. I desire that you may find as happy a home as theirs whenever you shall leave ours. Present Uncle the fairest Porter, spread the table for Miss Robie in your tastiest manner, and be your own best self all the time of your stay which I for my part desire may not be long.

Your affectionate
Father

All of the children adored their father as passionately as they did their mother. Abba was a devoted mother — it was a peculiarly devoted family — but Louisa was not for a long time as close to Bronson as he desired and he grieved about it. He knew with his unique prescience for children's needs that his second daughter had greater need for his influence than any of the others. But he would not urge her. She must come of herself. And it was not until her first great sorrow had come to her that Louisa turned to her father for help.

Abba gives us notice of the approach of this sorrow in a letter to Samuel May. When Elizabeth was seventeen, she had an attack of scarlet fever from which she was too long in recovering. Finally, Abba took her to the seashore, where this was written :

STEPHENS COLLEGE
LIBRARY

MRS. ALCOTT

Dear Brother: . . . Elizabeth's condition from day to day has left me in doubt what to write about her. The first week was warm and pleasant and the change was grateful to her . . . but the last weeks have been cold and rainy and most unfortunate to her. Dr. Newhall thinks it best to remove her directly back, that the comforts of home and the society of the family are now all important to her. Dr. Charles gives a different opinion, that she has in every way failed but that she has not even incipient disease of the lungs and that a week of fine weather may produce a most salutary effect. So I shall remain until next month. . . . It seems to me that the system of medicine is a prolonged guess. The change of scene has been very beneficial to me. The very sight of the ocean has restored me to a sense of individual power. . . .

> Your affectionate Abba.

Another letter, three months later

> Concord, Dec. 8, 1857.

Dear Sam:

. . . Give my love to dear Joseph and tell him poor Elizabeth can sympathize with him in this protracted feebleness. She gains a little but is almost insupportably emaciated. Her condition is most peculiar. I try to be hopeful both for her sake and Mr. Alcott's. . . . Louisa brings her downstairs in her arms occasionally but she is glad to get back to the quiet and privacy of her own room. . . . We have nice letters from Mr. Alcott. He is doing well (in his lectures) at Rochester. We are, all the rest of us at home, taking care by turns of Elizabeth. The girls are about to give a tea party for the anti-slavery cause — they have given two dramatic benefits. Louisa in Mrs. Pontifec was irresistible. She brought down the house in a storm of laughter, she looking unmoved. Abby takes drawing lessons and works steadily. Anna is all care for mother and sick sister, for the neatness of the house, etc. . . . There is to be an anti-slavery meeting, shortly. Hope I shall be able to have them here, some of them, but it must depend on my baby.

Yours, Abba.

Concord, January 21, 1858

My dear Brother: I have just now only time and heart for a few facts. We have sent for Mr. Alcott at Cleveland, — expect him home tomorrow. Dr. Geist pronounces Elizabeth's case hopeless. . . . She has failed rapidly lately, sees that dissolution is near, is calmly quiet, cheerful, awaits the great change which shall relieve her misery. I can lay no purer offering on the Altar of the Lord than this gem of the Spirit. I have struggled to save her for the past year, but sometimes before our greatest peace comes our greatest strife. And now I feel that my darling will be in safer hands than her mother's.   She wrote in my Journal that beautiful Hymn of aspiration by Miss Flower —

"Nearer, my God to thee, nearer to thee,
  E'en though it be a cross, that raiseth me . . ."

You shall hear from me soon again.
        God bless you, dear.
                                Yrs, Abba.

                    Concord, March 19, 1858

My dear Brother :
    In the anguish of a bereaved heart we are apt to cry out for help.   We seek sympathy and renewed demonstrations that our friends are with us in our trouble.   The last week has found me each successive day hugging to my own soul the destitution of my being and refusing to be comforted by any outward help, but summoning all the quiet beauty of Elizabeth's character and imbibing for my present strength all the holy spirit which pervaded her last suffering hours.   I dare not dwell on the fever which I conveyed to my home, which devoured the dear freshness of her life.   I dare not dwell on the helplessness of science. . . .   The fact is before me.   She has faded like a shadow through the valley of death into life and light. . . .   On Sunday the 14th at 3 o'clock, she sweetly closed her eyes.   On the Friday evening before she reached out her arms to her father, and said, "Take me,

273

father, into your lap." He did so. . . . The girls, seeing something unusually serene about us, closed in the group. She smiled at each one. "*All* of us here." She put a stray bleached lock of her father's hair, behind her ear. "How beautiful! Air! Air!" The window was opened. "Heavenly air. I go, I go. Lay me down gently." We did so. . . . Then she slept. . . . On Sunday morning at once I called Anna from the couch and sent her upstairs for Louisa and Abby. We watched the slow receding of all that was mortal until three o'clock. Louisa and I lay her dressed on the couch. The girls went to bed and Mr. Alcott and I sat down to try to bring home the lesson. . . . On Monday, Dr. Huntingdon came up at three P.M. and read the Chapel Service. A neighbor or two who sing very sweetly chanted "Come ye Disconsolate" (Elizabeth's favorite tune) to which I joined both in heart and voice, "Earth has no sorrow that Heaven cannot heal." Mr. Emerson, Sanborn, Thoreau and John Pratt bore her across the threshold and placed her in the carriage. . . . It has been an intense Lent, a long Passion week. May the stone be rolled from the grave of my affections that I may live again to do my duty.

Ever, Abby

It was the first rift in the family. Mrs. Alcott, who, by visiting a poor family afflicted with scarlet fever, had brought the disease to Elizabeth, suffered as only an intense nature like hers could suffer. Anna, with her father's deeply philosophical nature, was to a certain extent sufficient to herself, but Louisa, ardent, tempestuous, could find comfort nowhere in her own soul and at last went to her father.

Louisa was a woman now. She was very tall, only a little under six feet and finely proportioned. Her rich chestnut hair was caught back from her face by a velvet band, showing her dark eyes heavy with weariness and pain. She had not yet come into her own. She was slow in the making. The turbulent nature had needed long years of discipline before coming to its best, just as her father had foreseen when he wrote in his diary of the baby girl who was so difficult to handle.

Louisa found her father in the garden. He had been raking up the beds, for it was April now and the robins had come again. When Louisa reached his side, he was resting on a bench under an apple tree. His face was a little drawn, but his eyes were serene.

"Father!" exclaimed Louisa, dropping to the bench beside him. "Father, can you help me? The sleepless nights are wearing me out."

Bronson took one of the strong young hands between his own and chafed it. "Poor Lu!" he said. "How can I help you, dear?"

"Father! Where is Beth now? Does she only lie rotting there in Sleepy Hollow? Oh, I can't bear the thought of it!"

Her father kissed her, then looked slowly about the April garden and across the road to the April meadows, just flushed with green. "I wonder," he said slowly, "if I can make you see life as I see it. I've tried to, ever since you were a baby. But you've always preferred your mother's philosophy. Hers is brave and fine and you were quite right to choose as you wished. But, one cannot come to this faith of mine in a moment. One grows to it, with the years, as Anna has. I wonder . . ."

Again he paused to study the fields and the sky.

Louisa gave a little sob. "I want to comfort mother. And I cannot."

"When you and Anna were born," he said, "I started and kept a journal about you, for I thought then that I had great things to tell the world about childhood. I planned to do the same for Elizabeth, but by the time I was ready to begin with her I had discovered that the world would not listen

276

STEPHENS COLLEGE
LIBRARY

L O U I S A

to my ideas about education. . . . Elizabeth
was the loveliest of all our babies. She had
the most extraordinarily ethereal type of beauty.
There was something so angelic about her that
she inspired me to write about her as typifying
the immortal soul. Psyche, you remember, was
a lovely maid who personified immortality."

"Yes," said Louisa. "Of course, I know the
one of your Journals labeled 'Psyche.'"

"Also," added Bronson with the humorous lift
to his lips, "you never have had time to read it
through or ponder its pages. . . . Well," with a
little sigh, "you are only like the rest of the world
in that and I cannot blame you. Yet, now you
come to me with a question that I tried to answer
around Elizabeth's infancy. I have been reading
parts of that journal over and over again since
her death. Perhaps I can find passages that will
help you."

He lifted the old Diary from the bench. "Psyche,
1838." He turned the yellowed leaves and read,
"Observe the child. At the age of seven he casts
off his entire foetal body. He has a new body.
His first has passed away. He has buried his
primal skin and bone. And yet amidst this change
of his outer garmnet, this advent and departure

of substance, he is the same, identical nature. He abides.

"And the change proceeds every seven years, typifying itself in childhood, adolescence, maturity, completing the cycle in dotage. Nurturing itself to retrace the same steps until it shall cast off its corporeal envelope to resume it no more. For in such wise do birth and death, beset and accompany the soul through every step of its bodily sojourn. Yet does the soul hold fast to its vital identity through all such mutation and trans-substantiation.

"Verily the soul builds and wastes its own structures. But yet, nothing perishes. Nothing wastes. All is ceaseless mutation, transfiguration. Form alone changes. Essence abides. The soul transfigures its own visage. . . . Matter yields to the hand of the Spiritual Potter. It renews while wasting.

"Spirit! 'T is the architect of nature. It builds her temples. It moulds her bodies. Life is its work. It clothes itself in Nature then anon it casts aside its robe. . . . Forms vanish. The arch of nature gives way. There is no footway across the stream of Time. Then again, Spirit rebuilds the bridge, and the terrestrial sojourner proceeds on his way to the bourne of immortality.

"Aged is the soul. Behold her type in nature. Watch her in the recurring seasons. She lives too in these and is a party to their changes. But years and days as typified by them do not mark the soul's chronology. Centuries and milleniums are but historic ciphers denoting the soul's transit across Time.

"Yet Psyche never waxes old." Bronson paused as he read these words. "Psyche — Elizabeth," he murmured, "I cannot separate the two in my mind. . . . She never waxes old. She renews and quickens all things. . . . She defies all mutation. She wakes and configures all change. Quick and believing, she clothes all things with her own greenness nor does aught wax old in her faith. Constant to her trust, she grows young as time passes over her nor can winter nor change take aught from her dewy freshness. She never casts her spring time or doffs her childhood. She passes through all changes, herself unchanged.

"And in the last terrestrial hour, like a child sinking softly into sweet and hopeful slumber on the maternal bosom, does she lay herself confidingly in the arms of nature and passes away immortal into the arms of decay. She enters the domain of the Ancient of Days, there to behold with Him both the Evening and the Morning Stars. She observes the cycle of years. She renews the perpetuity of her Being in the Heart of God. . . ."

Bronson closed the book.

Tears were running unchecked down Louisa's

cheeks. "Read it to me again, Father," she whispered.

Again in his beautiful voice he read the words that Elizabeth's death had rendered profoundly significant to him. When he had finished, Louisa tucked the book under her arm. "It will be like touching Beth to have it with me," she said. "I want mother to hear it."

"You must not thrust it on your mother," said Bronson slowly. "She has her own strong way of working out her problems. You must not confuse her self-reproaches with lack of faith. She has her own faith."

"But not yours!" Louisa spoke in her quick way.

"Not mine. We agreed after Fruitlands that we loved each other so greatly that mentally we dared each to go our own way."

"Mother's way," said Louisa, "is the way of many other people, while you, except perhaps for Mr. Emerson, have gone alone. I wish —" Louisa looked with sudden and new understanding at the fine, thought-worn face beside her, "I wish I 'd taken your hand and gone with you, sometimes. Mother could have spared me. You must have had a sort of — of world loneliness that I 've never understood — till now — now that dear Beth's death and these words you 've read me have — have given me understanding."

A smile of extraordinary sweetness lighted Bronson's face. He laid his hand on Louisa's shoulder. "It's not too late, my dear. With Anna going to her beloved John, and Elizabeth gone, perhaps you could go on brain excursions with me, occasionally, without neglecting your dear mother."

"Indeed I can!" exclaimed Louisa. "How proud I 'll be! I have n't Anna's sheer intellect or Elizabeth's serenity — but —"

"But," her father interrupted, "you have the gift of words and a superb driving power. I have great faith that while the world has refused the children of my brain, that the children of my body, it will find equipped for its finest uses. Perhaps now that our dear Elizabeth has shown you the way to me, you will let me help you to think the thoughts you want to think."

He looked at Louisa with pathetic wistfulness.

"Oh, if you only will!" she cried. "I am so tired of floundering!"

For answer he laid his cheek caressingly against hers.

The little boy of Spindle Hill had come a long and tragic way since the winter's afternoon when in the old kitchen, under his mother's direction, he had written A a, B b, on the floor. And he was to know no higher, sweeter moment in his life than this. While to Louisa, holding the worn Journal, "Psyche, 1838" against her heart, there came anew the conviction that her father was tremendous and that she was a thousand times blessed in that she was permitted to draw from his deeps to slake her thirsty soul.

So they sat gazing on the greening April fields.

THE END

BIBLIOGRAPHY

Unpublished Journals of Bronson Alcott.

Unpublished Journals and Letters of Anna, Abba Elizabeth, May and Mrs. Alcott.

Unpublished Correspondence of Bronson Alcott.

Autobiography of Margaret Fuller Ossili. 1852, Boston.

"Society in America." Harriet Martineau, 1837, London.

"A Retrospect of Western Travel." Harriet Martineau, 1838, London.

"Record of a School." Elizabeth P. Peabody, 1835, Boston.

"Conversations on the Gospels (1836–1837)." Bronson Alcott, reported by Elizabeth Peabody, Margaret Fuller, Sophia Peabody (Mrs. Nathaniel Hawthorne). Boston.

"Transcendental Wild Oats." Louisa May Alcott. Boston.

"Memoir of Bronson Alcott." F. B. Sanborn. Boston, 1893.

"Letters and Journals of Ralph Waldo Emerson." Boston.

"New Connecticut." Bronson Alcott. 1851.

مصر[؟]

ببغاء